FOLLOW the
PROPHETS

Cover image: *Family Portrait* © Chihhang

Cover design copyright © 2013 by Covenant Communications, Inc.

Published by Covenant Communications, Inc.
American Fork, Utah

Printed in the United States of America
First Printing: January 2013

20 19 18 17 16 15 14 13   10 9 8 7 6 5 4 3 2 1

ISBN-13: 978-1-62108-324-5

FOLLOW the PROPHETS

52 FHE LESSONS FROM LATTER-DAY PROPHETS

REBECCA K. IRVINE

Covenant Communications, Inc.

TABLE OF CONTENTS

INTRODUCTION

Your family can hold uplifting and fun family home evenings every week of the year with these quick and easy lessons based on the lives of latter-day prophets. *Lessons from Latter-day Prophets* tutors families using memorable stories, proven teaching strategies, and clear concepts that will better help loved ones live the gospel. Week after week, lesson after lesson, children and parents alike will look forward to sharing time together as you become a forever family.

Follow the Prophets: 52 Family Home Evening Lessons from Latter-day Prophets was written to help families teach basic gospel principles and significant events in Church history. At least three different FHE lessons are included for each of the sixteen latter-day prophets, each lesson touching on significant personal incidents that prophet experienced and the major impact he had on the Church. Also included for each prophet is a brief biographical sketch, a list of important dates, a coloring page illustration, and several fun activities. There are fifty-two interesting and uplifting lessons in all—one for each week of the year.

HOW TO USE THIS BOOK

1. REVIEW the lessons for each prophet and decide in which order you want to teach them. Since there are lessons about gratitude (Thanksgiving), fathers (Father's Day), a Christ-centered life (Christmas), and patriotism (Independence Day), you may choose to teach in other than chronological order.

2. DELEGATE teaching responsibilities to each family member before each lesson. You'll find a suggested scripture, music selections, and activities for each lesson. Children are more likely to remember the lessons if they are involved and help teach.

3. PRINT and COPY the coloring page or activity pages as provided for the lesson. The CD-ROM that accompanies this book contains the activity pages for every lesson. The answer key at the end of the book provides answers to appropriate activity pages.

4. ENJOY the lessons and time shared together in FHE studying what we learn from the lives of our latter-day prophets.

5. DISPLAY the pictures of the prophets in a prominent location in your home to remind family members of the lessons you have learned together in FHE.

Joseph Smith Jr.

CHAPTER ONE
JOSEPH SMITH

Introduction (2 Ne. 3:11–13)

The very first prophet of the latter days was Joseph Smith.
Born December 23, 1805, to Joseph Smith Sr. and Lucy
Mack Smith, Joseph was an outgoing and athletic boy. He
worked hard on his father's farm growing up, but always
enjoyed having fun. As a young man Joseph Smith was called
as a prophet and directed to restore the true gospel of Jesus
Christ to the earth. He did so, establishing The Church of
Jesus Christ of Latter-day Saints on April 6, 1830. In addition
to restoring the Church, Joseph's greatest accomplishments
include the restoration of priesthood authority and power to
the earth, the translation and publication of scripture (the
Book of Mormon, Doctrine and Covenants, and the Bible),
and the restitution of temple ordinances. During his lifetime
Joseph saw the Church grow from a small handful to more
than 26,000 members.

Joseph Smith's Testimony of Christ

"And now, after the many testimonies which have been given
of him, this is the testimony, last of all, which we give of
him: That he lives! For we saw him, even on the right hand
of God; and we heard the voice bearing record that he is
the Only Begotten of the Father—That by him, and through
him, and of him, the worlds are and were created, and the

inhabitants thereof are begotten sons and daughters unto God." (D&C 76:22–24)

Important Dates and Events in the Life of Joseph Smith:

Birth—December 23, 1805, in Sharon, Vermont

Parents—Lucy Mack and Joseph Smith Sr.

Baptism—May 15, 1829 (age 24)

Marriage—January 18, 1827, to Emma Hale

Children—11 (6 died in infancy, 2 were adopted)

Called as an Apostle—June 1829 (age 23)

Ordained Prophet—April 6, 1830 (age 24)

Years as Prophet—14 years, 2 months

Death—June 27, 1844, in Carthage, Illinois

Lesson 1: Joseph's Leg Operation

Purpose: To help family members learn the importance of holding true to personal standards, even in the face of trials

Gospel Principles: Faith, diligence, and endurance

Scripture: D&C 66:9

Music: "Press Forward" (*Hymns*, no. 81), "Faith" (CS, 96)

Lesson:

At the age of seven, Joseph Smith needed to have surgery on his left leg because typhus fever had settled in his shin. Twice a doctor came and drained the swollen leg to help Joseph recover, but after each procedure his leg got worse. Several surgeons who came and looked at Joseph's leg concluded the infection had gone all the way into the bone and that his leg should be amputated. Joseph's mother begged them not to amputate but to try a new surgery they had mentioned where only the dead part of the bone would be removed. After some debate, the doctors agreed to try the new procedure. Joseph refused liquor to deaden the pain, and instead of being bound to the bed he asked his father to hold him during the surgery. He also asked his mother to leave the house so she would not hear his cries. The surgery was performed successfully and Joseph immediately began to recover.

Activities:

1. Print a copy of "Activity Page 1.1: Joseph's Expression of Faith" from the CD-ROM. After completing the activity page, discuss how family members can exercise greater faith in challenges they may experience.

2. Create an obstacle course using everyday items such as trash cans, pillows, chairs, and other household items.

Blindfold one family member. Assign a person who can see to navigate the blindfolded person through the obstacle course. Take turns letting other family members go through the obstacle course. At the end of the game, talk about how this is the type of faith required when a person trusts his or her life to God.

Additional Resources:

1. A cartoon-illustrated version of this story, "An Operation on Joseph's Leg," was published in the *Liahona*, February 2008, F10–F11.

2. A flannel board version of this story is available for use and is found in "Joseph Smith's Operation," *Friend*, February 2008, 48.

3. See also Lucy Mack Smith, *History of Joseph Smith*, ed. Preston Nibley (Salt Lake City: Deseret Book Company, 1979), 54–58.

Lesson 2: The First Vision

Purpose: To help family members learn that God answers prayers and to help build personal testimonies of Joseph Smith as a prophet of God

Gospel Principles: Prayer, revelation, and personal testimony

Scripture: JS—H 1:10–17

Music: "Joseph Smith's First Prayer" (*Hymns*, no. 26), "The Sacred Grove" (CS, 87)

Lesson:

When he was fourteen years old, Joseph Smith witnessed a religious revival in the area where his family lived. Many Christian preachers taught things that seemed to conflict, which was very confusing to Joseph. Because of his confusion, Joseph wanted to know which church was right and which church he should join. As he searched for answers, he opened the Bible to James 1:5, where he read, "If any of you lack wisdom, let him ask of God, that giveth to all men liberally, and upbraideth not; and it shall be given him." This verse struck him with great force and he decided to pray to God to ask which of the many churches he should join. In a grove of trees near his home, where he could speak privately in prayer, Joseph knelt to ask God. While praying, a pillar of light descended upon him. "When the light rested upon me I saw two Personages, whose brightness and glory defy all description, standing above me in the air. One of them spake unto me, calling me by name and said, pointing to the other 'This is My Beloved Son. Hear Him!'" (JS–H 1:17).

Activities:

1. Print a copy of "Activity Page 1.2: First Vision Crossword Puzzle" from the CD-ROM. Work on the puzzle as a family to review the lesson concepts.

2. For younger children, use the finger puppets included in the Nursery manual[1] or the flannel board illustrations published in the March 2008 *Friend* and have the children take turns retelling the story of the First Vision.

3. For older children, complete the crossword puzzle together; have family members take turns providing answers to each clue.

Additional Resources:

Illustrations of the First Vision are included in the Gospel Art Kit (Church History pictures 402 and 403). "The Restoration" DVD (2005, 54742091) is an excellent and easy way to teach family members about the First Vision.

---

[1]"Lesson 21: Joseph Smith Saw Heavenly Father and Jesus Christ," *Behold Your Little Ones: Nursery Manual* (2008), 88–91.

Lesson 3: The Golden Plates

Purpose: To help family members learn details about the coming forth of the Book of Mormon and gain a testimony of this book of scripture

Gospel Principles: Prayer, obedience, and scriptures

Scripture: JS—H 1:34, 42

Music: "Come, Listen to a Prophet's Voice" (*Hymns*, no. 21), "An Angel Came to Joseph Smith" (CS, 86a)

Lesson:

On September 21, 1823, the angel Moroni visited seventeen-year-old Joseph Smith and told him about an ancient record, kept on gold plates, that was buried in the Hill Cumorah near Joseph's home. Moroni said that Joseph would need to get the plates and translate them but that many would try to take the plates from him. The next day Joseph went to the place he was shown by Moroni but was told it was not yet time to get the plates. Over the next four years Joseph went to Cumorah once a year and was taught by Moroni that the gospel was being restored to the earth. Finally, Joseph was allowed to take the plates from the stone box hiding place in 1827. Over the next two years, Joseph worked on translating the ancient record with the help of several different scribes. The translation was finally completed in late June 1829, and the first edition of the Book of Mormon was printed in March 1830.

Activities:

1. Print a copy of "Activity Page 1.3: Golden Plates Seek and Find" from the CD-ROM. Pair up family members to play this game or hold a tournament to see who can win overall.

2. Use aluminum foil to make family members their own "plates" on which to write. To make the plates, fold a large piece of foil in half; fold it in half again to make small book-sized pages. Punch holes for rings to go through the pages. Have family members use a pencil, crochet hook, or other blunt object to write their feelings about the gospel on the "plates." Use rings to hook all the "plates" together.

Additional Resources:

1. Gospel Art Kit pictures 404, 406, and 416 are illustrations associated with the visits of the angel Moroni and of the translation work that took place on the Book of Mormon.

2. A flannel board story, "Joseph Smith Receives the Gold Plates," is available in the *Friend*, May 2008, 48.

3. Six mini-coloring pages tell the story of the coming forth of the Book of Mormon in "Coming Forth of the *Book of Mormon*," *Friend*, September 2004, 24–25.

Lesson 4: The Kirtland Temple

Purpose: To help family members learn more about the important role temples play in the plan of salvation

Gospel Principles: Building temples, temple work, sacrifice

Scripture: D&C 105:33

Music: "How Beautiful Thy Temples, Lord" (*Hymns*, no. 288), "I Love to See the Temple" (CS, 95)

Lesson: The command to build the first temple in the latter days was given to the Prophet Joseph Smith in January 1831, less than a year after the Church was organized. At the time, the Church was very small and had little money, but the Saints began the work and looked forward to the promised blessing of being "endowed with power from on high" in the temple (see D&C 38:32). Great sacrifices were made by Church members to build the temple. They gave of their time, talents, money, and even their personal possessions. Crushed pieces of glass and pottery were mixed into the stucco, which gave the exterior of the temple a sparkly appearance in the sun. It took five years of hard work and sacrifice, but the Saints were able to complete the Kirtland Temple and dedicate it to the work of the Lord on March 27, 1836.

Activities:

1. Print a copy of "Activity Page 1.4: Eyewitnesses at the Kirtland Temple Dedication Puzzle" from the CD-ROM. Put the puzzle together as a family and discuss what it might have been like to have been at the dedication of the Kirtland Temple.

2. Memorize the lyrics to the hymn, "The Spirit of God" (*Hymns*, no. 2). Written by William W. Phelps in anticipation

of the dedication of the Kirtland Temple, the words accurately reflect the spirit of Pentecost witnessed on that occasion.

3. Go on a scavenger hunt to gather objects representing ways in which the early Saints sacrificed and worked to build the Kirtland Temple. Some possible items to collect might include a rock, white fabric (to represent the curtains), a glass object (broken glass was in the mortar), a needle, cornmeal, play money, building tools, and a watch/clock (to represent time). After all the items are collected, discuss how each of the items represents something the pioneers sacrificed to help build the temple.

Additional Resources:

1. A fun fictional story about the Kirtland Temple was published in the July 2002 *Friend* (Sheila Kindred, "Laying the Cornerstone," 4).

2. Bake some Nauvoo pioneer gingerbread cookies like the ones sold by the Scovil Bakery in Nauvoo. Ingredients: 1/2 C. white sugar, 1/2 C. molasses, 1/3 C. oil, 1/3 C. water, 1 egg, 3 1/2 C. all-purpose flour, 1/2 tsp. baking soda, 1/4 tsp. salt, 1/2 tsp. cinnamon, and 1/2 tsp. ground ginger. Directions: In a large bowl, mix the sugar, molasses, oil, and water. Beat in the egg. In a separate bowl, stir all the dry ingredients. Add the dry ingredients to the wet ingredients until thoroughly combined. Shape the dough into 1" balls and place them on a greased cookie sheet. Bake at 350° F (175° C) for 8–12 minutes. For added fun, cut them out in the shape of the Nauvoo Temple.[2]

---

[2] *"Kitchen Krafts," Friend*, July 1993, 23.

Lesson 5: The Death and Martyrdom of Joseph Smith

Purpose: To help family members understand the circumstances surrounding the death of Joseph Smith and to strengthen testimonies of Joseph as a prophet of God

Gospel Principles: Loyalty, Church governance, obedience

Scripture: D&C 135:1

Music: "Praise to the Man" (Hymns, no. 27), "Latter-day Prophets" (CS, 134)

Lesson:

Many times the Prophet Joseph was falsely accused and arrested for crimes he did not commit. On June 25, 1844, Joseph, his brother Hyrum, and a few other Church leaders turned themselves in to officials at Carthage Jail in answer to a warrant for treason. A trial date was set for June 29 and Joseph was to stay in jail until the trial. Although there was trouble keeping the prisoners safe, Illinois Governor Thomas Ford disregarded requests for help. Shortly after five o'clock on June 27, an angry mob of more than two hundred men gathered outside the jail. The mob rushed the jail and shots were fired. Shot in the face, Hyrum was the first to die. Joseph was killed just minutes later, falling from the second-story window after being shot multiple times. John Taylor—who was saved from a bullet by his pocket watch—and Willard Richards both survived the attack. Although the Prophet Joseph Smith died, the work of the Lord has continued. Joseph sealed his testimony with his blood, and the Lord has continued to call new prophets to lead the Church in these latter days.

Activities:

1. Print a copy of "Activity Page 1.5: Martyrdom True or False Trivia Quiz" from the CD-ROM.

2. As a family, go to http://josephsmith.net; under **Historical Sites**, click **Illinois**. In the multimedia section, review the Carthage Jail photographs, illustrations, and maps for a visual tour of Joseph Smith's and Hyrum Smith's final days.

Additional Resources:

1. Read John Taylor's eyewitness account of the death of the Prophet Joseph Smith in the *History of the Church* (*DHC* 7:99–108).

2. A dot-to-dot picture of Joseph Smith's profile that could also be colored was published in the October 2002 *Friend*.

Brigham Young

CHAPTER TWO
BRIGHAM YOUNG

Introduction (2 Ne. 3:11–13)

Born in Vermont in 1801, Brigham Young was the third youngest of eleven children born to John and Abigail Young. He grew up in the densely forested lands of central New York, where he learned to work hard. At age sixteen, Brigham became an apprentice carpenter and enjoyed learning what he felt was "honest, reliable work, such as would endure." In 1824 (at age twenty-three) he married Miriam Works, but she died eight years later of tuberculosis. In 1834 Brigham married again—this time to Mary Ann Angell.

As the second prophet in the latter days, Brigham Young is known as the "Lion of the Lord" because he was fearless in proclaiming the truth. He once said he wanted the "tongue of seven thunders to wake up the people"[3] and call them to repentance—and with his strong teaching style, he often did so. One of President Young's most common themes was the importance of seeking the Spirit and communicating with the Lord in prayer. Brigham Young is also famous for his work as a colonizer. He had great vision and encouraged the Saints to be productive and self-sufficient. Brigham Young helped ensure the Church would prosper and grow as the kingdom

---

[3] Brigham Young and John Widtsoe, *Discourses of Brigham Young* (Salt Lake: Deseret Book, 1954), 18:304.

of God on the earth. He died at age seventy-six on August 29, 1877.[4]

Brigham Young's Testimony of Jesus Christ

"I testify that Jesus is the Christ, the Saviour and Redeemer of the world; I have obeyed His sayings, and realized His promise, and the knowledge I have of Him, the wisdom of this world cannot give, neither can it take away."[5]

Important Dates and Events in the Life of Brigham Young:

Birth—June 1, 1801, in Whitingham, Vermont

Parents—Abigail Howe and John Young

Baptism—April 14, 1832 (age 30)

Mission—Ohio, New York, Ontario (1832–1833); Great Britain (1839–1841)

Marriage—October 5 or 8, 1824, to Miriam Works (first wife)

Children—56 (10 died in infancy)

Called as an Apostle—February 14, 1835 (age 33)

Ordained Prophet—December 27, 1847 (age 46)

Years as Prophet—29 years, 8 months

Death—August 29, 1877, in Salt Lake City, Utah

---

[4] "With 'The Tongues of Seven Thunders'," *Liahona*, April 1998, 26.
[5] *Deseret News Weekly*, October 11, 1876, 582 (as quoted in Richard Neitzel Holzapfel and William W. Slaughter, *Prophets of the Latter Days* [Salt Lake City: Deseret Book, 2003], 2).

Lesson 1: Brigham Young's Conversion and Baptism

Purpose: To help family members understand the principles of study and prayer in finding truth and in receiving personal revelation to gain a testimony

Gospel Principles: Faith, scripture study, baptism

Scripture: Isa. 29:7, D&C 9:7–9

Music: "Come Follow Me" (*Hymns*, no. 116), "Baptism" (*CS*, 100)

Lesson:

In April 1830, Brigham Young's brother, Phinehas, met Samuel Smith, who was laboring as a missionary in Mendon, Vermont. Smith was soon introduced to the rest of the Young family. A copy of the newly printed Book of Mormon was loaned to Phinehas, who then shared it with other family members. Later, a second copy was also provided to the family by Elder Smith. A few of Brigham's brothers and sisters read it and quickly gained a testimony of its truthfulness, but Brigham was more cautious. "'Hold on,' says I. . . . 'Wait a little while; what is the doctrine of the book, and of the revelations the Lord has given? Let me apply my heart to them.' . . . I examined the matter studiously, for two years, before I made up my mind to receive that book. I knew it was true, as well as I knew that I could see with my eyes, or feel by the touch of my fingers, or be sensible of the demonstration of any sense. Had not this been the case, I never would have embraced it to this day."[6] Brigham Young was finally baptized in his own mill stream by Elder Eleazar

---

[6] Address delivered by Brigham Young on August 8, 1852, contained in the *Journal of Discourses*, vol. 3.

Miller in April 1832. On that special occasion, he felt a powerful witness of the Spirit testifying his sins had been forgiven. All of Brigham's brothers and sisters, as well as his father, were also baptized that same day. His wife, Miriam, was baptized three weeks later.[7] The Young family members remained faithful for the remainder of their lives.

Activities:

1. Print a copy of "Activity Page 2.1: If or If Not" from the CD-ROM. After sharing the story of Brigham Young's conversion and baptism, complete the activity page and reveal the key to Brigham's testimony.

2. Play the dictionary game: Use a dictionary to select uncommonly used words. Write down the correct definition for the word as well as two other fake definitions. During FHE, read the word and then have family members select which definition is the correct one. After playing this game, discuss how it is sometimes hard to identify those things that are true. Have family members list ways that we can learn truth (answers could include prayer, scripture study, promptings of the Holy Ghost, and so on).

3. Make copies of the coloring page, "How Can I Gain a Testimony?"[8] Let children color the page as you discuss which of the actions Brigham Young took to help gain his testimony.

---

[7] "Chapter 1: The Ministry of Brigham Young," *Teachings of Presidents of the Church: Brigham Young*, 1.
[8] "How Can I Gain a Testimony?" *Friend*, November 2005, 35.

Additional Resources:

1. A more detailed account of Brigham Young's conversion was written by W. Jeffrey Marsh and published in the *Journal of Book of Mormon Studies,* Volume 10, issue 2. It can also be found online under the publications portion of http://maxwellinstitute.byu.edu.

2. BYU's website has a detailed biographical account of Brigham Young, including information on his youth and conversion; access it at http://unicomm.byu.edu/about/brigham.aspx.

3. The DVD segment "A Man Without Eloquence" (on the Church History collection DVD—item 54116000, available in most meetinghouses) recounts Brigham Young's conversion to the gospel.

Lesson 2: Becoming the Prophet

Purpose: To help family members learn that God chooses who will lead His Church

Gospel Principles: Line of succession, Holy Ghost, personal revelation

Scripture: Deut. 18:18

Music: "Come, Listen to a Prophet's Voice" (*Hymns*, no. 21), "Follow the Prophet" (CS, 110, chorus only)

Lesson:

After the death of the Prophet Joseph, Sidney Rigdon believed that because he had been in the First Presidency, it was his right to be the next leader of the Church; he was able to convince some people to agree with him. As the president of the Quorum of the Twelve, Brigham Young told the apostles all that mattered was what the Lord wanted and they should seek out His guidance. At a meeting of the Church to settle the matter, both Sidney Rigdon and Brigham Young spoke to the congregation. While Brigham Young spoke, a miracle happened: he suddenly looked and sounded like Joseph Smith to those in the audience. More than one hundred people at the meeting had this spiritual confirmation of Brigham Young as the next leader of the Church and made record of it in their journals. Zina Huntington said of this experience: "President Young was speaking. It was the voice of Joseph Smith—not that of Brigham Young. His very person was changed. . . . I closed my eyes. I could have exclaimed, I know that is Joseph Smith's voice! Yet I knew he had gone."[9] Wilford Woodruff

---

[9] Diantha Huntington Young, *Diaries 1844–1845*, August 8, 1844, holograph, LDS Church Archives, published in Maureen Ursenbach Beecher, "All Things Move in Order in the City: The Nauvoo Diary

declared, "If I had not seen him with my own eyes, there is no one that could have convinced me that it was not Joseph Smith speaking."[10] From 1844 to 1847, Brigham Young led the Church as the president of the Quorum of the Twelve Apostles. He was sustained as prophet while at Council Bluffs, Iowa, in December 1847.[11]

Activities:

1. Print a copy of "Activity Page 2.2: Brigham Young Appears to Be Like Joseph Smith" from the CD-ROM. Let family members create their own puppets. Take turns letting each retell the story in the lesson using his or her puppets.

2. Blindfold a family member and have him or her listen to voices of the other family members in the room (some may try to mask or disguise their voices; this is okay). See if the blindfolded person can guess who is speaking. Take turns letting other family members be blindfolded. Discuss how voices are often unique and that we can identify others by their voices. Note that this is what happened when Brigham Young both sounded and looked like Joseph Smith.

---

of Zina Diantha Huntington Jacobs," *BYU Studies* 19, no. 3 (1979), 285–320.

[10] Susan Arrington Madsen, *The Lord Needed a Prophet* (Salt Lake City: Deseret Book, 1990), 32.

[11] "Lesson 38: Brigham Young Leads the Church," *Primary 5: Doctrine and Covenants: Church History* (1997), 216.

3. Discuss how the death of a prophet is now handled so that family members can understand policies and procedures associated with the order the Lord has established in His Church.

Additional Resources:

1. A picture puzzle coloring page was published on page 5 of the February 1993 *Friend*. This page also includes a list of important dates and events in Brigham Young's life.[12]

2. An excellent *Ensign* article on ways Brigham Young learned from Joseph Smith was published in February 1998.[13] The article also includes details of how Brigham Young often felt guided by Joseph's spirit.

---

[12] "Brigham Young," *Friend*, February 1993, 5.
[13] Ronald W. Walker, "Brigham Young: Student of the Prophet," *Ensign*, February 1998, 51.

Lesson 3: Leading the Saints West

Purpose: To help family members learn about the gathering of the Saints in the early days of the Church

Gospel Principles: Pioneers, gathering to Zion, endurance

Scripture: D&C 136:1–16

Music: "Come, Come Ye Saints" (*Hymns*, no. 30), "The Handcart Song" (CS, 220)

Lesson:

After the death of Joseph Smith, the Saints were forced to leave Illinois. Under Brigham Young's leadership, they began a hard journey west. After spending some time at Winter Quarters, Brigham led a scouting party to the Salt Lake Valley, reaching the valley on July 24, 1847, when he famously stated, "This is the right place." Brigham Young had seen the valley in a vision and recorded in his journal, "The spirit of light rested upon me and hovered over the valley, and I felt that there the Saints would find protection and safety."[14] After reaching the Great Salt Lake, he then returned to Council Bluffs to begin directing the Saints further west. Slightly fewer than 100,000 Saints crossed the plains under President Young's direction before the railroad was finished in 1869, and the gathering continued even afterward. The Perpetual Emigration Fund made it possible for many to travel to Zion who may not have otherwise had the means. Once they arrived in Salt Lake, many were asked to leave and colonize approximately four hundred settlements in Utah and other surrounding states.[15]

---

[14] *Journal History,* July 23, 1847

[15] "Chapter 1: The Ministry of Brigham Young," *Teachings of Presidents of the Church: Brigham Young,* 1.

Activities:

1. Print a copy of "Activity Page 2.3: This is the Right Place Game" from the CD-ROM. After the lesson, play the game as instructed in the directions.

2. Gather several stories of pioneers crossing the plains; if possible, include a story of an ancestor who was a pioneer. Have each family member share a story.

3. For your FHE treats, offer traditional pioneer fare, such as berries, jerky, corn bread, johnnycakes, cheese, and so on.

Additional Resources:

1. Gospel Art Kit pictures 412, 414, 415, and 418 depict the Saints crossing the plains.

2. This is the Place Heritage Park in Salt Lake City is a great resource for teaching family members about Brigham Young leading the Saints west.

3. The Church-produced film *Legacy* (item number 54333090) tells the story of pioneers crossing the plains.

Lesson 4: The Salt Lake Temple

Purpose: To help family members learn about the history and importance of the Salt Lake Temple.

Gospel Principles: Temple work, work, trials

Scripture: D&C 95:8

Music: "How Firm a Foundation" (*Hymns*, no. 85), "Families Can Be Together Forever" (*CS*, 188)

Lesson:

Four days after the first Mormon pioneers entered the Salt Lake Valley, Brigham Young pointed out where the temple would be built, stating, "Here we will build a temple to our God." However, it would take more than five years of building homes, farming the land, and helping more pioneers cross the plains before construction could be started on the temple. The cornerstone of the foundation was finally laid on April 6, 1853, and the Salt Lake Temple was begun. A setback occurred when cracks in the sandstone foundation were discovered. These cracks made the foundation too weak to support the granite temple. Brigham Young had the temple foundation replaced with quartz from Little Cottonwood Canyon so the temple would last into the millennium. Although the Salt Lake Temple was not finished during Brigham Young's lifetime, he did have the privilege of seeing the dedication of the St. George Temple early in the year he died.

Activities:

1. Print a copy of "Activity Page 2.4: Salt Lake Temple Matching Game" from the CD-ROM. Match the important dates and events for construction of the Salt Lake Temple.

2. Use blocks, paper cups, or even cards to demonstrate the importance of building on a solid foundation. Show that structures will collapse when a foundation fails or is removed. After doing so, tell the story of the cracked Salt Lake Temple foundation and discuss why Brigham Young made the decision to replace it with one of granite. Ask family members if they think this was a difficult decision for Brigham Young to make.

Additional Resources:

1. Visit Temple Square and the model of the interior of the Salt Lake Temple displayed in the South Visitors' Center.

2. As a family, watch the Church-produced DVD *Mountain of the Lord*, which details the construction of the Salt Lake Temple (item number 54300090). Portions of this video are available online.

John Taylor

CHAPTER THREE
JOHN TAYLOR

Introduction (Mosiah 13:20)

As the only latter-day prophet not born in America, John Taylor lived his early life in the beautiful country of England. From his earliest days, he had a strong belief in God and often prayed, even while working in the fields, and continued his fervent Bible study after being apprenticed to a carpenter. In his youth, John had a vision of an angel blowing a trumpet and was so in tune with the Spirit that he often heard soft strains of heavenly music. John had the prompting as a young man that someday he needed to preach in America. While living in Toronto, Canada, John Taylor and his wife met with a religious study group several times a week. Together they sought to find truth through study and prayer but did not know of any church that truly followed the gospel pattern established by the Savior while He was on the earth. The Lord heard their prayers, and soon Parley P. Pratt arrived as a missionary. John Taylor was intrigued by Parley P. Pratt and wrote down many of the sermons Elder Pratt taught so that he might compare the teachings of the Church to the Bible. After three weeks of serious study and prayer, John Taylor was convinced of the truthfulness of the Church; both he and his wife, Leonora, were baptized on May 9, 1836. Soon after, President Taylor was called to serve as the presiding officer in Canada.

John Taylor's Testimony of Jesus Christ

"Jesus came here according to the foreordained plan and purpose of God, pertaining to the human family as the Only Begotten of the Father full of grace and truth. He came to offer himself a sacrifice, the just for the unjust; to meet the requirements of a broken law, that the human family were incapable of meeting, to rescue them from the ruins of the fall, to deliver them from the power of death to which all peoples had been subjected by the transgression of a law."[16]

Important Dates and Events in the Life of John Taylor

Birth—November 1, 1808, in Milnthorpe, England

Parents—Agnes and James Taylor

Baptism—May 9, 1836 (age 27)

Mission—England (1840–1841, 1846); France and Germany (1850–1851); New York (1854–1856)

Marriage—January 28, 1833, to Leonora Cannon (first wife)

Children—34

Called as an Apostle—December 19, 1838 (age 30)

Ordained Prophet—October 10, 1880 (age 71)

Years as Prophet—6 years, 9 months

Death—July 25, 1887, in Kaysville, Utah

---

[16] *Deseret News Semi-weekly,* July 9, 1881, 1.

Lesson 1: "Defender of the Faith"

Purpose: To help family members recognize the importance of standing up for their beliefs and exercising faith in the Lord

Gospel Principles: Courage, integrity, missionary work

Scripture: D&C 9:7–9

Music: "True to the Faith" (Hymns, no. 254), "Dare to Do Right" (CS, 158)

Lesson:

John Taylor is often called the "Defender of the Faith," a nickname he earned over and over again in his lifetime. Once, after first visiting Kirtland to meet the Prophet Joseph Smith, President Taylor heard some of the local members speaking negatively about the Prophet. John quickly defended the Prophet and told the members they needed to look to Joseph to follow the Lord, just as the children of Israel needed to follow Moses to get through the wilderness. Another time in Ohio, John Taylor courageously faced down an unfriendly congregation that planned to tar and feather him. Tearing open his vest, he boldly offered himself as their victim but when no one came forward, he began to preach the restored gospel to them. Later, some in the congregation apologized to him for their harmful intentions.

Activity:

Print a copy of "Activity Page 3.1: Defenders of the Faith Word Find" from the CD-ROM. As you search for the names of prophets, discuss how each acted in defense of his faith. For example, Daniel defended his faith by refusing to follow a law that said he could not pray. After finding all the prophets' names, discuss ways family members may need to defend their beliefs in real life.

Additional Resources:

1. Lesson 13 of the manual *Presidents of the Church* discusses John Taylor as a "Defender of the Faith"[17] (available online at www.lds.org).

2. The story told in this lesson is available in cartoon format in the August 2003 *Friend*.[18]

3. A puzzle of John Taylor to cut out and assemble is available in the February 1993 *Friend*.[19]

---

[17] "Lesson 13: John Taylor—Defender of the Faith," *The Presidents of the Church: Teacher's Manual*, 57.
[18] "From the Life of President John Taylor," *Friend*, August 2003, 44–45.
[19] "John Taylor," *Friend*, February 1993, 35.

Lesson 2: John Taylor at the Martyrdom

Purpose: To help family members learn more about the martyrdom of Joseph Smith through the eyes of John Taylor as an eyewitness

Gospel Principles: Prophets, music, trials

Scripture: Deut. 18:18

Music: "We Thank Thee, O God, for a Prophet" (*Hymns*, no. 19), "Stand for the Right" (CS, 159)

Lesson:

John Taylor was one of the three men with Joseph Smith in Carthage Jail when a mob stormed the upstairs room, killing the Prophet and his brother, Hyrum. With his beautiful baritone voice and at the request of the Prophet, Elder Taylor sang "A Poor Wayfaring Man of Grief" twice just before the mob attacked. Hyrum and Willard Richards tried to hold the door closed as the first wave of men rushed up the stairs. Hyrum was quickly shot in the face and died almost instantly. As Brother Richards tried to keep the door shut, John Taylor tried to deflect the blasting gun muskets being thrust through the narrow opening. But his efforts were in vain. The Prophet was shot more than a dozen times and fell from the window. Elder Taylor was also shot multiple times. The one shot that might have killed him was stopped by his pocket watch. The Lord had preserved John Taylor's life for a greater work.

Activities:

1. Print a copy of "Activity Page 3.2: A Poor Wayfaring Man of Grief" from the CD-ROM. After filling in all the blanks, sing the song as a family. Discuss why this song might have comforted Joseph Smith in Carthage Jail.

2. Have a family member dress up and pretend to be John Taylor, giving his eyewitness account of what happened in Carthage Jail. Use D&C 135 as supplement text if needed.

3. If possible, visit the historic Carthage Jail and Visitors' Center in Carthage, Illinois, which offers free tours. You can find details about visiting the site at www.historicnauvoo. net; the site also provides a brief summary of the mob attack that killed Joseph and Hyrum Smith. Those unable to visit in person may find a visit to the website a worthwhile substitute.

Additional Resources:

1. Use the *Primary 5* lesson manual for further tips and activities related to John Taylor's experience at Carthage Jail.[20]

2. "John Taylor: Witness to the Martyrdom of the Prophet Joseph Smith"[21] is a scholarly article detailing John Taylor's eyewitness account of the martyrdom. Utilize this article when teaching older children or adults; it is available online at http://rsc.byu.edu/archived/champion-liberty-john-taylor.

---

[20] "Lesson 37: Joseph and Hyrum Smith Are Martyred," *Primary 5: Doctrine and Covenants: Church History* (1997), 210.
[21] Mark H. Taylor, "John Taylor: Witness to the Martyrdom of the Prophet Joseph Smith," in *Champion of Liberty: John Taylor*, ed. Mary Jane Woodger (Provo, UT: Religious Studies Center, Brigham Young University, 2009), 45–63.

Lesson 3: Missionary Service

Purpose: To help family members learn the sacrifices and efforts John Taylor made to share the gospel as a missionary

Gospel Principles: Missionary work, faith, sacrifice

Scripture: D&C 136:1–16

Music: "Called to Serve" (*Hymns*, no. 249), "We'll Bring the World His Truth" (CS, 172)

Lesson:

John Taylor was one of the Church's most effective early missionaries. He served three different missions, the first two in Great Britain and a third in France and Germany. Upon leaving for his first mission with Wilford Woodruff, John Taylor was sick and penniless and left behind a wife who was seriously ill. Despite these stresses, John set forth without any complaints. He had great faith his wife would get well and money would be provided by the Lord as necessary throughout his mission. Along the way, the Lord took care of John Taylor by prompting people—many times complete strangers—to give him assistance. Even the passage of him and his companion across the Atlantic Ocean was paid by donations from others.

Another way John Taylor defended and shared the gospel was through writing and publishing. He was the author of numerous Church pamphlets and served as editor of the early Church newspapers *Times and Seasons* and *Nauvoo Neighbor*. Brigham Young once described John Taylor as "one of the strongest editors that ever wrote." President Young had such confidence in John Taylor's writing and editing talents that he called him to go to New York City to organize and publish a newspaper (*The Mormon*) that could help to accurately inform people about the Church. Later, while serving his mission to France and Germany, Elder Taylor was able to publish the Book of Mormon in French and German. John Taylor's talents as a writer and editor helped many people have a greater understanding of the restoration of the gospel.

Activities:

1. Print a copy of "Activity Page 3.3: The *Nauvoo Neighbor*" from the CD-ROM. Have each family member write a brief newspaper article or cut out a picture from a Church magazine to include.

2. Compose a "family" testimony of the gospel and place it in the front of a copy of the Book of Mormon. Give it to a friend or family member or send it to a full-time missionary to give away.

Additional Resources:

1. You might want to read the article by Paul Thomas Smith in the *Ensign* that gives additional detail regarding John Taylor's mission to the British Isles.[22]

2. A cartoon version of John Taylor's work as a missionary can be found in the *Friend*.[23]

---

[22]Paul Thomas Smith, "Among Family and Friends: John Taylor—Mission to the British Isles," *Ensign*, March 1987, 37.
[23]"From the Life of President John Taylor," *Friend*, June 2003, 42–43.

3. To read some of John Taylor's writings, check out *John Taylor Nauvoo Journal*, which was re-released in 1996,[24] or *The Gospel Kingdom: Selections from the Writings and Discourses of John Taylor*.[25]

---

[24] John Taylor, *John Taylor Nauvoo Journal*, ed. Dean C. Jessee (Provo, Utah: Grandin Books, 1996).

[25] *The Gospel Kingdom: Selections from the Writings and Discourses of John Taylor*, comp. by G. Homer Durham (Salt Lake City: Bookcraft, 1943).

Wilford Woodruff

CHAPTER FOUR
WILFORD WOODRUFF

Introduction (Mosiah 2:22)

Wilford Woodruff was raised in Connecticut by his father and stepmother; his mother died when Wilford was only fifteen months old. Wilford went to school, played with friends, and worked hard on his family's farm. However, while growing up, President Woodruff had a remarkable number of accidents—most of which could have taken his life. For example, he was chased by an angry bull; nearly thrown from a horse onto a steep, rocky mountainside; broke both his legs and arms in different incidents; and was "drowned, frozen, scalded, and bit by a mad dog."[26] Despite all of these accidents, Wilford Woodruff's life was preserved and he lived to become the fourth prophet of the Church in these latter days. He is best known for keeping his journal, overseeing the completion of the Salt Lake Temple, and receiving the revelation ending the practice of plural marriage.

Wilford Woodruff's Testimony of Jesus Christ

"I always have had faith in the Bible and in the revelations of God since I was a boy like these sitting on these seats, eight or ten years old, when I went to the Presbyterian Sunday

---

[26] "The Life and Ministry of Wilford Woodruff," *Teachings of Presidents of the Church: Wilford Woodruff*, xviii.

School and read about Jesus Christ. I believed then that he was the Saviour of the world; I believed that the Old and New Testament was true. I believe it today."[27]

Important Dates and Events in the Life of Wilford Woodruff

Birth—March 1, 1807, in Farmington, Connecticut

Parents—Beulah Thompson and Aphek Woodruff

Baptism—December 31, 1833 (age 26)

Mission—Southern States (1834–1836); Eastern States/Fox Islands (1837–1838); Great Britain (1839–1841)

Marriage—April 13, 1837, to Phoebe Carter (first wife)

Children—33

Called as an Apostle—April 26, 1839 (age 32)

Ordained Prophet—April 7, 1889 (age 82)

Years as Prophet—9 years, 4 months

Death—September 2, 1898, in San Francisco, California

---

[27] *Deseret News Weekly,* July 21, 1875, 388 (as quoted at http://www.lds.org/churchhistory/presidents).

Lesson 1: Missionary Service

Purpose: To help family members learn about the dedication required to be in the service of God as a missionary

Gospel Principles: Missionary work, faith, obedience

Scripture: D&C 4

Music: "Go Forth with Faith" (*Hymns*, no. 263), "I Want to Be a Missionary" (CS, 169)

Lesson:

Wilford Woodruff was one of the earliest missionaries for the Church, serving at least four different full-time missions. His first mission was to the southeastern United States. Although he had little funds or supplies and no companion, he willingly went and served the Lord. At the end of this mission he had journeyed more than 9,800 miles, most of it on foot. Wilford's second mission was to the Fox Islands off the coast of Maine. While serving this mission, he learned he had been called to the Quorum of the Twelve Apostles. Shortly after that he was called, along with a number of the other apostles, to preach the gospel in Great Britain. Woodruff's greatest missionary success stemmed from his work among the six hundred members of the United Brethren while in England. He wrote in his journal that they converted "all the United Brethren save one."[28] Because of these missionary efforts, many Church members trace their pioneer roots to Wilford Woodruff.

---

[28] "Lesson 15: Wilford Woodruff—Faithful and True," *The Presidents of the Church: Teacher's Manual*, 69.

Activities:

1. Print a copy of "Activity Page 4.1: Missionary Badges" from the CD-ROM. Have family members wear the badges during the lesson. Encourage them to prepare for serving missions by being member missionaries now.

2. Show family members a world map. Ask where they would most like to visit or serve a mission. Place markers on these locations, then place additional markers on the places where Wilford Woodruff served missions (should include: southeastern United States [1835–1836]; Farmington, Connecticut [1837]; Fox Islands, Maine [1837]; Great Britain [1839]; and the European Mission [1844], where he served as president).

Additional Resources:

1. The Mormon history blog, www.keepapitchinin.org, published an eighteen-part series of illustrated experiences Wilford Woodruff had on his first mission to the southeastern United States.

2. "Harvest in Herefordshire" is an interesting *Ensign* article detailing missionary experiences of Wilford Woodruff.[29]

3. The *Friend* has published a story about Wilford Woodruff's Benbow Farm missionary experience.[30]

---

[29] David J. Whittaker, "Harvest in Herefordshire," *Ensign*, January 1987, 46.

[30] Paula Hunt, "Conversion at the Benbow Farm," *Friend*, June 1995, 3.

Lesson 2: Journal Keeping

Purpose: To help family members recognize the importance of and blessings that come from keeping a personal journal

Gospel Principles: Journal writing, diligence, record keeping

Scripture: 3 Ne. 27:23–25

Music: "Home Can Be a Heaven on Earth" (*Hymns*, no. 298), "I Want to Live the Gospel" (CS, 148)

Lesson:

In the course of his lifetime, Wilford Woodruff had the opportunity to serve as both assistant Church historian (for more than twenty-five years) and as Church historian (for about six years). However, many feel President Woodruff's greatest contribution to LDS Church history was the records he kept in his own personal journals. From the earliest days of his conversion, Wilford Woodruff kept a daily record of his life, Church activities, and other important occurrences. In fact, President Woodruff noted he felt like a "fish out of water" until he had written in his journal each day.[31] His journal entries—more than seven thousand pages in all—give valuable insight into the day-to-day workings of the Church and provide record of great discourses given by Joseph Smith and other Church leaders.

---

[31] "The Life and Ministry of Wilford Woodruff," *Teachings of Presidents of the Church: Wilford Woodruff*, 125.

Activities:

1. Print a copy of "Activity Page 4.2: Journal Jar Writing Prompts" from the CD-ROM. Cut out the prompts and place them in a small jar, box, or envelope. Use the thirty topics as needed or to help develop a regular habit of journal writing over the course of a month.

2. If family members do not currently have journals, purchase inexpensive composition books and spend time decorating the covers with craft paper, stickers, ribbons, or other fun items.

Additional Resources:

1. *Banner of the Gospel: Wilford Woodruff* (2010) is a selection of presentations from the annual BYU Church History Symposium hosted by BYU Religious Education to honor Wilford Woodruff and to celebrate the two-hundredth anniversary of his birth.

2. A cartoon-illustrated story of Wilford Woodruff's journal keeping was published in the *Friend*.[32]

---

[32] "Keeping a Record," *Friend*, November 2006, 44–45.

Lesson 3: Temple Work

Purpose: To help family members understand and appreciate the importance of doing family history and temple work for the dead

Gospel Principles: Temple work, righteous leaders, redeeming the dead

Scripture: D&C 137:7–9

Music: "The Day Dawn is Breaking" (*Hymns*, no. 52), "Genealogy—I Am Doing It" (*CS*, 94)

Lesson:

As prophet, Wilford Woodruff spent much of his time as an advocate of temple work. He was the prophet who was finally able to dedicate the Salt Lake Temple but one of his most sacred temple experiences involved a vision he had in the St. George Temple of the founding fathers of the United States. Of this experience, he said, "Before I left St. George, the spirits of the [Founding Fathers] gathered around me, wanting to know why we did not redeem them. Said they, 'You have had the use of the Endowment House for a number of years, and yet nothing has ever been done for us. We laid the foundation of the government you now enjoy, and we never apostatized from it, but we remained true to it and were faithful to God.' These were the signers of the Declaration of Independence, and they waited on me for two days and two nights. . . . I straightway went into the baptismal font and called upon Brother McCallister to baptize me for the signers of the Declaration of Independence, and fifty other eminent men, making one hundred in all, including John Wesley, Columbus, and others."[33] Under President Woodruff's direction, additional temple work was done for more than six hundred prominent men and women in history.[34]

Activities:

1. Print a copy of "Activity Page 4.3: Profiles of Distinguished Men and Women" from the CD-ROM. Have family members color the pictures; as an alternate activity, make two copies of each profile and use as a memory game. Read and discuss the quotes on each of the profiles.

2. Make plans to attend the temple to do baptisms for the dead as a family. If possible, bring your own family names.

Additional Resources:

1. "Wise Men Raised Up" is an *Ensign* article giving details about the Founding Fathers.[35]

2. *The Other Eminent Men of Wilford Woodruff*, by Vicki Jo Anderson (Zichron Historical Research Institute, 1994), gives brief histories of men who appeared to Wilford Woodruff in the St. George Temple.

---

[33] *Journal of Discourses*, 19:229

[34] Wilford Woodruff, Journal, 7:367–369 (as quoted in Glen W. Chapman, *Vision of Former Eminent Men in the St. George Temple*, compiled January 2002, .pdf file located at http://chapmanresearch. org).

[35] Frank W. Fox and LeGrand L. Baker, "Wise Men Raised Up," *Ensign*, June 1976, 27.

Lorenzo Snow

CHAPTER FIVE
LORENZO SNOW

Introduction (Acts 17:28)

Lorenzo Snow was the fifth president of The Church of Jesus Christ of Latter-day Saints, serving for three short years (from 1898 to 1901). Born on April 3, 1814, the oldest son of Oliver and Rosetta Pettibone Snow, Lorenzo was a hard worker, both on his family's farm and in school. He was baptized in Kirtland, Ohio, at age twenty-two, following in the footsteps of several other family members who had been converted. Prior to his time as prophet, Lorenzo served many missions for the Church, including service in England, Italy, and the Pacific, as well as in the southern and northwestern United States. President Snow is particularly famous for his saying, "As man now is, God once was: As God now is, man may be."[36] One of his biggest challenges as prophet was that the Church was suffering under a crushing weight of debt. President Snow reiterated the necessity of tithe-paying among the Saints to help get the Church solvent again.

Lorenzo Snow's Testimony of Jesus Christ

"As long as memory continues and reason shall assert its throne, I never can permit the powerful testimony and knowledge that was communicated to me to remain silent.

---

[36] "Chapter 5: Lorenzo Snow," *The Presidents of the Church*, 88.

It was revealed to me. The heavens were opened over my head, and the power of God and the light of the Holy Ghost descended and elevated my whole being, and gave me the most perfect knowledge that Jesus was the Son of God. It was not the result simply of opinion or belief, as is the case in many other things, but it was a knowledge far beyond that of belief or opinion. I knew that God had sent His angels and restored the fullness of the Gospel as taught in ancient times; that He sent angels to authorize Joseph Smith, and gave him authority to administer in the ordinances of the Gospel, and to promise the Holy Ghost to all who would be obedient."[37]

Important Dates and Events in the Life of Lorenzo Snow

Birth—April 3, 1814, in Mantua, Ohio

Parents—Rosetta Leonora Pettibone and Oliver Snow

Baptism—June 19, 1836 (age 22)

Mission—Ohio (1837), Missouri/Ohio (1838–1839), England (1840–1843)

Marriage—April 21, 1845, to Sarah Ann Prichard (first wife)

Children—42

Called as an Apostle—February 12, 1849 (age 34)

Ordained Prophet—September 13, 1898 (age 84)

Years as Prophet—3 years, 1 month

Death—October 10, 1901, in Salt Lake City, Utah

---

[37] *Millennial Star,* April 18, 1887, 242.

Lesson 1: Lorenzo Snow's Life Is Preserved

Purpose: To help family members learn that the Lord protects those who are in His service

Gospel Principles: Prayer, inspiration, miracles

Scripture: 1 Ne. 5:8

Music: "When Faith Endures" (*Hymns*, no. 128), "Tell Me the Stories of Jesus" (*CS*, 57, third verse)

Lesson:

On an official trip to Hawaii with Joseph F. Smith and William Cluff, Lorenzo Snow's life was miraculously saved. Upon arriving, the three needed to leave the steamer and take a smaller boat to the shore. However, Joseph F. Smith declined to go, saying that the waters were too choppy and dangerous. Despite this danger, Lorenzo and Elder Cluff decided to venture ahead but while they crossed the offshore reef their boat was capsized. Lorenzo's body was found partially under the boat and he appeared to have drowned. Elder Cluff later described how hard they worked to resuscitate him, all the while praying for aid from above. He wrote, "Finally we were impressed to place our mouth over his and make an effort to inflate his lungs, alternately blowing in and drawing out the air, imitating, as far as possible, the natural process of breathing. . . . After a little, we perceived very faint indications of returning life. . . . These grew more and more distinct, until consciousness was fully restored."[38]

---

[38] "Chapter 5: Lorenzo Snow," *The Presidents of the Church*, 2005, 83.

Activities:

1. Print a copy of "Activity Page 5.1: Miracles of the Sea" from the CD-ROM. Read scripture stories related to prophets who were blessed or protected from stormy seas. Discuss how the Lord blesses and protects leaders when they are on an errand for Him.

2. Download a coloring page of a ship on a stormy sea and make a copy for each family member. Have family members color the picture as they listen to the story of President Lorenzo Snow's life being saved.

3. Teach the principles of CPR and practice on a doll or dummy. Instructions are readily available online. Learning CPR is one of the requirements for Scouting and is also helpful for Young Women Personal Progress (see Knowledge value 7).

Additional Resources:

1. Gospel Art Kit picture 421 is of a ship and could be used to illustrate the above story.

2. A puzzle coloring page of Lorenzo Snow to cut out and assemble was published in the April 1993 *Friend*.[39]

---

[39] "Lorenzo Snow," *Friend*, April 1993, 5.

Lesson 2: A Vision of the Savior

Purpose: To help family members build a stronger testimony of the Savior and of the sacredness of the temple as the house of the Lord

Gospel Principles: Jesus Christ, testimony, temples

Scripture: Moro. 10:32

Music: "I Believe in Christ" (*Hymns*, no. 134), "If the Savior Stood Beside Me" (available on www.lds.org[40])

Lesson:

President Lorenzo Snow's granddaughter Allie was once with him in his office in the Salt Lake Temple. It was nighttime, and President Snow was walking Allie to the front entrance as she was on her way home. While passing through the large hallway leading to the celestial room, Lorenzo stopped his granddaughter and said, "Wait a moment, Allie, I want to tell you something. It was right here that the Lord Jesus Christ appeared to me at the time of the death of President Woodruff. He instructed me to go right ahead and reorganize the First Presidency of the Church at once and not wait as had been done after the death of the previous presidents, and that I was to succeed President Woodruff." Then President Snow took the time to describe to Allie the glory of the Savior, describing His hands, feet, and even His clothing. Allie also recalled President Snow testified to her, saying: "Now, grand-daughter, I want you to remember that this is the testimony of your grand-father, that he told you with his own lips that he actually saw the Savior, here in the Temple, and talked with Him face to face."[41]

[40] Sally DeFord, "If the Savior Stood Beside Me," *Friend*, October 1993, 1.

[41] LeRoi C. Snow, "An Experience of My Father's," *Improvement Era*,

Activities:

1. Print a copy of "Activity Page 5.2: Prophets Who Have Seen the Lord" from the CD-ROM. Take turns having family members look up the scripture references and match them to the correct prophets.

2. Visit a local temple. Point out to family members the phrase *House of the Lord* on the exterior of the temple. Discuss how the temple is special as a sacred place for the Lord to come when He visits the earth.

3. Have family members write in their journals how they might feel if they were able to see the Savior in person. With whom might they want to share this experience? Why did President Snow share this experience with his granddaughter?

Additional Resources:

1. A good article summarizing many of Lorenzo Snow's life experiences, including seeing the Savior, was published in the May 1993 *Liahona*.[42]

2. The experience President Snow had in the temple is included as part of a lesson in the Primary 1 manual.[43] This lesson contains some additional activities appropriate for younger children.

September 1933, 677 (as quoted in "Chapter 5: Lorenzo Snow," *The Presidents of the Church*, 85).

[42] Arthur R. Bassett, "Lorenzo Snow: Decisions of a Young Man," *Liahona*, May 1993, 26.

[43] "Lesson 26: Families Can Be Together Forever," *Primary 1: I Am a Child of God* (2000).

Lesson 3: Tithes and Offerings

Purpose: To help family members recognize the importance of paying tithes and offerings

Gospel Principles: Tithing, offerings, faith

Scripture: D&C 119:4

Music: "Because I Have Been Given Much" (Hymns, no. 219), "I Want to Give the Lord My Tenth" (CS, 150)

Lesson:

One of the major problems facing the Church when Lorenzo Snow became prophet was debt. The Church was deeply in debt and had little income to help pay off the loans. President Snow prayed and fasted much over the financial position of the Church. In early May 1899, the Lord revealed to President Snow that he and others of the leading brethren should go to St. George, Utah, and hold a conference. The first session of the conference in St. George was held on May 17, 1899. As the conference started, President Snow told the Saints that the Lord had not yet revealed to him why he was there. However, a short time later the Spirit came over him and he had a vision. President Snow said that he could see, as he had never seen before, how the law of tithing had been neglected by the people. He promised the Saints that if they observed strict obedience to the law of tithing, the Church would become free of its obligations and the Latter-day Saints would become a prosperous people. President Snow also explained that, "The time has now come for every latter-day Saint, who calculates to be prepared for the future and to hold his feet strong upon a proper foundation, to do the will of the Lord and to pay his tithing in full."[44]

---

[44] "Chapter 5: Lorenzo Snow," The Presidents of the Church, 87.

Activities:

1. Print a copy of "Activity Page 5.3: Tithing Box" from the CD-ROM. Have family members color the box then cut out the pattern and glue it together.

2. With younger children, practice paying tithing. Demonstrate by giving each child a bag of small candies; have children give one candy to tithing for every ten. Practice filling out a tithing form and placing it in the envelope. Role-play giving tithing envelopes to a member of the bishopric.

3. Have family members discuss the many things tithing is used for in the Church. Use the list of items for a game of charades.

Additional Resources:

1. There are numerous lessons about tithing in Sunday School, Primary, and other Church manuals (see, for example, Lesson 29 of the *Preparing for Exaltation: Teacher's Manual*[45]).

2. *Windows of Heaven* is a video depiction of Lorenzo Snow's revelation to have the Saints be more faithful in paying tithing. This DVD is available in most meetinghouse libraries (item 54116000).

---

[45] "Lesson 29: Paying Tithing with the Right Attitude," *Preparing for Exaltation: Teacher's Manual* (1998), 169.

Joseph F. Smith

CHAPTER SIX
JOSEPH F. SMITH

Introduction (D&C 138:11)

Joseph F. Smith was the first prophet born to LDS parents and raised in the Church. Born November 13, 1838, in Far West, Missouri, to Mary Fielding and Hyrum Smith, Joseph F. Smith was only five years old when his father and uncle, Joseph Smith, were martyred. As a boy, young Joseph helped his mother migrate to Utah with the Saints in 1848; they settled in Salt Lake City. However, four years later Joseph's mother passed away too; he was only thirteen years old at the time. By the time Joseph F. was fifteen he was called on his first mission, thus beginning a lifetime of service in the Church. He was called as an apostle at age twenty-seven and became prophet in 1901 (at age sixty-two). Under President Smith the Church acquired historic sites, built many meetinghouses, and expanded the use of educational academies and universities. He also oversaw a continued growth in Church membership, increasing from nearly 293,000 to 496,000 at the time of his death in 1918 (a 59 percent increase).

Joseph F. Smith's Testimony of Jesus Christ

"I know that my Redeemer lives. I feel it in every fiber of my being. I am just as satisfied of it as I am of my own existence. I cannot feel more sure of my own being than I do that my

Redeemer lives, and that my God lives, the Father of my Savior. I feel it in my soul; I am converted to it in my whole being. I bear testimony to you that this is the doctrine of Christ, the gospel of Jesus, which is the power of God unto salvation."[46]

Important Dates and Events in the Life of Joseph F. Smith

Birth—November 13, 1838, in Far West, Missouri

Parents—Mary Fielding and Hyrum Smith

Baptism—May 21, 1852 (age 13)

Mission—Sandwich Islands (1854–1857); Great Britain (1860–1863)

Marriage—May 5, 1866, to Julina Lambson (first wife)

Children—48 (5 adopted)

Called as an Apostle—July 1, 1866 (age 27)

Ordained Prophet—October 17, 1901 (age 62)

Years as Prophet—17 years, 1 month

Death—November 19, 1918, in Salt Lake City, Utah

---

[46] "I Know That My Redeemer Lives," *Improvement Era*, March 1908, 386.

Lesson 1: Gifts of the Spirit

Purpose: To help family members seek out the gifts of the Spirit in their own lives

Gospel Principles: Gifts of the Spirit, miracles, service

Scripture: D&C 46:8–26

Music: "Because I Have Been Given Much" (*Hymns*, no. 219), "I Feel My Savior's Love" (CS, 74)

Lesson:

At the age of fifteen, Joseph F. Smith was called in general conference to serve his first mission for the Church. He was sent to the Sandwich Islands (Hawaii), serving for four years until he was nineteen. Early on in his mission he was left alone in Kula, where he became ill; he described this experience as follows: "They [the Hawaiian people] had different habits to anything I had before known, and their food, and dress and houses and everything were new and strange. . . . For three months this seclusion from the world continued, but the history of that short period of my life never can be told. I had ample time to feel after the Lord and to draw near to him with my whole soul."[47] In less than three months in Kula, Elder Smith was blessed with the gifts of the Spirit, learned the language fluently, and grew to love the Hawaiian people. Joseph F. also became well known for his gift of healing and an ability to cast out evil spirits and was asked to preside over several different island branches during

---

[47] Joseph F. Smith, *From Prophet to Son: Advice of Joseph F. Smith to His Missionary Sons*, compiled by Hyrum M. Smith III and Scott G. Kenney (Salt Lake City: Deseret Book, 1981), i.

his mission. Upon completion of his service in 1857, Joseph
F. Smith returned to Utah but accepted a call just three years
later to serve another mission—this one to England. He
briefly served an additional mission to Hawaii in 1864.[48]

Activities:

1. Print a copy of "Activity Page 6.1: Gifts of the Spirit Word
Scramble" from the CD-ROM. Ask family members which
gifts of the Spirit they would most like to have in their lives.
Discuss what actions they may need to take, as did Joseph F.
Smith, to receive these gifts.

2. Before FHE, gather five gift bags along with enough of
the following for each family member: Smarties for wisdom
or knowledge, gum for prophecy, pretzels for tongues and
the interpretation of tongues, rocks for faith, and bandages
for healing and miracles. Place all of each gift item in a
gift bag. During FHE, have family members see what is in
each bag and try to guess which of the gifts of the Spirit are
represented by the items.

Additional Resources:

1. The article by Elder Robert D. Hales, "Gifts of the Spirit"
(*Ensign*, February 2002, 12), is a good overall description of
the role of the gifts of the Spirit.

2. For younger children, read "Gifts from God" (*Friend*,
March 2003, 36), which includes a craft activity.

---

[48] "The Life and Ministry of Joseph F. Smith," *Teachings of Presidents of
the Church: Joseph F. Smith*, xv.

Lesson 2: Vision of the Spirit World

Purpose: To help family members more fully understand missionary work in the spirit world

Gospel Principles: Spirit world, missionary work, redemption of the dead

Scripture: D&C 138:1–4

Music: "How Long, O Lord, Most Holy and True" (*Hymns*, no. 126), "Families Can Be Together Forever" (*CS*, 188)

Lesson:

Near the end of his life, President Joseph F. Smith received the revelation known as "the vision of the redemption of the dead," now found in D&C 138. While pondering the atoning sacrifice of the Lord, President Smith had had a vision of the Savior's visit to the spirit world prior to His resurrection. From this vision we learn that the righteous dead—including Adam and Eve and other well-known Biblical prophets—were assembled together in the spirit world, anxiously awaiting the Lord. During His visit there the Savior organized these "noble and great ones" to preach the gospel among the dead. Since then missionary work in the spirit world has continued so that all who did not have the blessings of the gospel during mortality may have the opportunity to accept it in the spirit world. President Smith spoke of this vision in his opening remarks at general conference on October 4, 1918. The vision was written shortly after conference and was presented to the Quorum of the Twelve Apostles, who unanimously accepted it as scripture.[49]

---

[49] "Chapter 6: Joseph F. Smith—Sixth President of the Church," *Church Presidents Student Manual*, 109 (see also *Teachings of Presidents of the Church: Joseph F. Smith*, xxiii).

Activities:

1. Print a copy of "Activity Page 6.2: Noble and Great Ones Matching Game" from the CD-ROM.

2. Have family members draw pictures of the Savior appearing to the Saints in the spirit world to organize missionary work. Ask, "Who do you think was there when the Savior appeared?" (read D&C 138:38-47, 55). Ask, "Who would you like to have as a mission companion if you were to serve a mission in the spirit world?"

Additional Resources:

1. Read more about D&C 138 from the Doctrine and Covenants Institute manual, which can be downloaded for free at http://institute.lds.org.

2. *Heirs of the Kingdom,* a 30-minute audio recording about D&C 138, is part of a series in which BYU Religious Education faculty members discuss the writings and teachings of the Doctrine and Covenants. Listen to it for free on the Internet at www.byub.org/doctrineandcovenants.rss.

3. Elder D. Todd Christofferson gave a talk entitled, "The Redemption of the Dead and the Testimony of Jesus," in the October 2000 general conference. Read the talk in the November 2000 *Ensign,* or listen to an audio recording of the talk on www.lds.org.

Lesson 3: Family Home Evening

Purpose: To help family members more fully understand and appreciate the importance of family home evening

Gospel Principles: Family, following the prophet, teaching in the home

Scripture: "Happiness in family life is most likely to be achieved when founded upon the teachings of the Lord Jesus Christ. Successful marriages and families are established and maintained on principles of faith, prayer, repentance, forgiveness, respect, love, compassion, work, and wholesome recreational activities" (*The Family: A Proclamation to the World*, paragraph 7).

Music: "Love At Home" (*Hymns*, no. 294), "Family Night" (CS, 195)

Lesson:

President Joseph F. Smith is well known for his influence in instituting the practice of family home evening in the Church. Compelled by his concerns for good family environments, teaching in the home, and the need to combat forces pulling homes apart, President Smith released a statement in 1915 urging the Saints to hold a weekly home evening that would help strengthen families and individuals. [50] Specifically, the statement noted:

"We advise and urge the inauguration of a 'Home Evening' throughout the Church, at which time fathers and mothers may gather their boys and girls about them in the home and teach them the word of the Lord. They may thus learn more fully the needs and requirements of their families; at

---

[50] "Chapter 6: Joseph F. Smith—Sixth President of the Church," *Church Presidents Student Manual*, 101.

the same time familiarizing themselves and their children more thoroughly with the principles of the Gospel of Jesus Christ. This 'Home Evening' should be devoted to prayer, singing hymns, songs, instrumental music, scripture-reading, family topics and specific instruction on the principles of the Gospel."

Additionally, the First Presidency promised that those Saints who followed this counsel would be blessed:

"If the Saints obey this counsel, we promise that great blessings will result. Love at home and obedience to parents will increase. Faith will be developed in the hearts of the youth of Israel, and they will gain power to combat the evil influences and temptations which beset them."[51]

Activities:

1. Print a copy of "Activity Page 6.3: Family Fun Nights Crossword" from the CD-ROM. After completing the crossword, select a few of the family home evening ideas in the puzzle and plan to incorporate them in upcoming weeks.

2. Read and discuss the following statements by the First Presidency about family home evening:

"We call upon parents to devote their best efforts to the teaching and rearing of their children in gospel principles which will keep them close to the Church. The home is the basis of a righteous life, and no other instrumentality can take its place or fulfill its essential functions in carrying forward this God-given responsibility. We counsel parents and children to give highest priority to family prayer, family

---

[51] *Teachings of the Presidents of the Church: Joseph F. Smith*, 241.

home evening, gospel study and instruction, and wholesome family activities."[52]

"Family home evenings should be scheduled once a week as a time for discussions of gospel principles, recreation, work projects, skits, songs around the piano, games, special refreshments, and family prayers. Like iron links in a chain, this practice will bind a family together, in love, pride, tradition, strength, and loyalty."[53]

"Our spiritual progress, individually and as a Church, will largely be determined by how faithfully we live the gospel in our homes. The most important calling of a priesthood holder is that of husband and father. The most divine station of woman is that of wife and mother. . . . Fathers should lead their families in holding meaningful family home evenings. Such experiences will build family unity and influence each person toward increased righteousness and happiness."[54]

Additional Resources:

1. *Famous Family Nights* (Cedar Fort, Inc., 2009) contains numerous fun and interesting personal FHE stories of famous LDS individuals.

2. The introduction of *Family Home Evening Adventures* (Horizon, 2009) shows families how to plan out an entire year's worth of family home evening lessons.

---

[52] First Presidency letter, 11 February 1999—Gordon B. Hinckley, Thomas S. Monson, and James E. Faust.

[53] Ezra T. Benson, "Salvation; A Family Affair," *Ensign*, July 1992, 4.

[54] *Family Home Evening*, 1980—Spencer W. Kimball, N. Eldon Tanner, and Marion G. Romney.

Heber J. Grant

CHAPTER SEVEN
HEBER J. GRANT

Introduction (Deut. 6:17–18)

As a young boy, Heber J. Grant was raised by his mother, Rachel, the widow of Jedediah Grant. More than once in his youth it was prophesied that Heber would become a great leader in the Church. By the time he was in his mid-teens he had been ordained a Seventy; at age twenty-three he was called to be a stake president; and at age twenty-five he was called to serve in the Quorum of the Twelve Apostles. As an apostle, Elder Grant was sent to Japan to open the first Japanese mission of Church; later he had the opportunity to preside over the British and European Mission. In 1918, after the death of Joseph F. Smith, Heber J. Grant was ordained as the prophet. During his thirty-seven years as prophet, he dedicated three new temples, enforced the Manifesto against plural marriage, and helped the Church cope with both the Depression and World War II. President Grant's business acumen and connections helped the Church on both a national and international level as never before.[55]

---

[55] "Heber J. Grant—Seventh President of the Church," Chapter 7, *Church Presidents Student Manual*, 110.

Heber J. Grant's Testimony of Jesus Christ

"Not only did Jesus come as a universal gift, He came as an individual offering with a personal message to each one of us. For each one of us He died on Calvary and His blood will conditionally save us. Not as nations, communities or groups, but as individuals."[56]

Important Dates and Events in the Life of Heber J. Grant

Birth—November 22, 1856, in Salt Lake City, Utah

Parents—Rachel Ridgeway Ivins and Jedediah Morgan Grant

Baptism—June 2, 1864 (age 7)

Mission—President of Japanese Mission (1901–1903); President of British and European Mission (1904–1906)

Marriage—November 1, 1877, to Lucy Stringham (first wife)

Children—12

Called as an Apostle—October 16, 1882 (age 25)

Ordained Prophet—November 23, 1918 (age 62)

Years as Prophet—26 years, 5 months

Death—May 14, 1945, in Salt Lake City, Utah

---

[56] "A Marvelous Growth," *Juvenile Instructor,* December 1929, 697.

Lesson 1: Determination and Diligence

Purpose: To help family members understand the blessings that can come from perseverance in the face of difficulty

Gospel Principles: Diligence, perseverance, faith

Scripture: D&C 103:36

Music: "When Faith Endures" (*Hymns*, no. 128), "Every Star Is Different" (CS, 142)

Lesson:

Although Heber J. Grant's life was not easy, he is well known for his perseverance. A favorite saying of President Grant's was, "That which we persist in doing becomes easier to do; not that the nature of the thing has changed, but our capacity to do has increased." Here are three stories illustrating President Grant's determination and diligence in the face of difficulty:

1. While growing up, Heber wanted to be on the baseball team that would win the Utah Territorial championship. However, none of the other boys wanted him on their team because he was unable to throw the ball from one base to another. Despite his physical weaknesses, Heber earned and saved money to buy a baseball with which he could practice. He spent hours throwing the ball against the bishop's barn wall as he tried to hone his skills. Eventually he was able to be on the winning baseball team for California, Colorado, and Wyoming.

2. With faith, diligence, and the Lord's help, Heber J. Grant overcame many challenges. For example, in his youth he set a goal to become a bookkeeper. Bookkeepers were required to have very good penmanship, though, and Heber did

not have this talent. In fact, many of his friends found fault with his sloppy writing, calling it "chicken scratches." But Heber was not put off. Instead, he simply began practicing his penmanship until it improved so much he was invited to teach penmanship at one of the local schools. He was also able to reach his goal of becoming a bookkeeper.[57]

3. Later in his life, Heber J. Grant set a goal to learn how to sing. Many people laughed at his voice when he sang because it was so out of tune. Some even said President Grant's singing sounded like someone getting their teeth pulled. Just as he did with baseball and handwriting, Heber began practicing to improve. Once as he traveled on a carriage to a conference in Arizona, he sang so much his companions pleaded with him to stop. But Heber continued practicing until eventually he was able to stay on tune when he sang his favorite hymns.[58]

Activities:

1. Print a copy of "Activity Page 7.1: Scrambled Proverbs" from the CD-ROM. Discuss the meanings of these common sayings in relation to persistence, diligence, and determination. Ask, "Do any of these sayings relate to President Grant's actions?"

2. Have a family competition using the three talents Heber J. Grant strived to develop. See who can throw the best strike, demonstrate the nicest penmanship, and sing a song completely in tune. Give an award to the family member who performs the best in each area or overall.

---

[57] Leon R. Hartshorn, "Heber J. Grant: A Man Without Excuses," *New Era*, January 1972, 45.
[58] Truman G. Madsen, *The Presidents of the Church* (Salt Lake City: Deseret Book, 2004), 191.

3. Ask family members to come to FHE prepared to share a talent. For example, they may sing or play an instrument, display a piece of artwork, recite a poem, tell a joke, or share an experience they had using their talents elsewhere.

Additional Resources:

1. Cartoon versions of Heber J. Grant's persistence in practicing baseball[59], learning to sing[60], and as a hard worker[61] have been published in the *Friend*.

2. Chapter 7 of the CES manual, *Presidents of the Church* (available online at www.ldsces.org), discusses the persistence and diligence of Heber J. Grant. Included in this chapter is a painting of President Grant as a boy throwing a baseball.

3. Numerous websites offer free, printable penmanship worksheets for practice, both in cursive and in printing.

---

[59] "From the Life of President Heber J. Grant," *Friend*, March 2004, 12–13.
[60] "From the Life of President Heber J. Grant," *Friend*, July 2004, 40–41.
[61] "From the Life of President Heber J. Grant," *Friend*, Oct. 2004, 30–31.

Lesson 2: The Curse of Debt

Purpose: To encourage family members to recognize the blessings that come from taking financial responsibility and living within their means

Gospel Principles: Self-reliance, preparedness, provident living

Scripture: D&C 104:78

Music: "Come, Ye Thankful People" (*Hymns*, no. 94), "For Thy Bounteous Blessings" (CS, 21)

Lesson:

Heber J. Grant went through both prosperous and lean times in his life. He experienced the chains of debt, both as a leader of the Church and in his personal life. In the 1890s President Grant lost $30,000 on an investment in a lumber company, another $30,000 on sheep, and a third $30,000 in a loan he had signed for a family member. These losses caused him to be in great personal debt but he refused to declare bankruptcy—he felt it was his duty to repay the money owed. He organized his family to work together to meet the obligations, which they were able to do with great patience and the Lord's help. Because of this experience, President Grant was better prepared to lead the Church through the Great Depression and was well known for urging the Saints to "Get out of debt, and stay out of debt."[62]

Activities:

1. Print a copy of "Activity Page 7.2: Heber J. Grant's Two Cents' Worth Puzzle" from the CD-ROM. Afterward, read the following quote to family members from the *All is Safely*

---

[62] Truman G. Madsen, *The Presidents of the Church* (Salt Lake City: Deseret Book, 2004), 188.

Gathered In pamphlet. Discuss how finances are important to spiritual safety. (Note: You can obtain a hard copy of the pamphlet from your bishop or ward library, or read the .pdf version of the pamphlet online at providentliving.org.)

"We encourage you wherever you may live in the world to prepare for adversity by looking to the condition of your finances. We urge you to be modest in your expenditures; discipline yourselves in your purchases to avoid debt. . . . If you have paid your debts and have a financial reserve, even though it be small, you and your family will feel more secure and enjoy greater peace in your hearts."[63]

2. Visit the provident living website (providentliving.org) and take the online finance course, "Peace in Your Heart: Managing Household Finances Wisely." Set a goal as a family to improve in at least one of the four areas discussed in the course (paying tithes, using a budget, avoiding debt, and building a reserve).

Additional Resources:

1. The provident living website (providentliving.org) has numerous other resources available for those interested in learning how to get out of debt or how to manage their finances. Take time to explore this helpful website.

2. There are numerous books that explain the intricacies of getting out of debt. Three of the bestselling books include Suze Orman's *The Money Book for the Young, Fabulous & Broke* (Riverhead Trade, 2007); Robert Kiyosaki's *Rich Dad, Poor Dad* (Business Plus, 2010); and Dave Ramsey's *The Total Money Makeover* (Thomas Nelson, 2009). These and many others are likely available at your local library.

---

[63] The First Presidency, *All Is Safely Gathered In: Family Finances,* February 2007, 1.

3. Several nonprofit services are available to help advise those burdened by debt. American Consumer Credit Counseling, for example, is just one nonprofit credit counseling agency that helps consumers take control of their financial lives through credit counseling, debt consolidation, and financial education. Do a web search for services available in your local area.

Lesson 3: Word of Wisdom

Purpose: To teach family members the importance of living the Word of Wisdom as a way to help them have a healthy body and spirit

Gospel Principles: Word of Wisdom, health, obedience

Scripture: D&C 89:18–21

Music: "True to the Faith" (Hymns, no. 254), "The Word of Wisdom" (CS, 154)

Lesson:

Although the Word of Wisdom was introduced in the earliest days of the Church, compliance with this commandment was erratic among the Saints until the early part of the twentieth century. Heber J. Grant and Joseph F. Smith encouraged Church members to make the Word of Wisdom a central part of living the gospel. President Grant knew first-hand that addictions to coffee and alcohol were not good for the body or the spirit: A close personal friend of his, a returned missionary, died at a young age due to cirrhosis of the liver after living a life addicted to alcohol. Seeing this tragedy, President Grant promised the Lord he would be an enemy of alcohol and tobacco from that time forward. He counseled the Saints to avoid these addictive substances so they could receive promised blessings. And in 1921, Heber J. Grant made observance of the Word of Wisdom a requirement to receive a temple recommend.[64]

---

[64] "Chapter 21: Observing the Word of Wisdom," Teachings of Presidents of the Church: Heber J. Grant, 189.

Activities:

1. Print a copy of "Activity Page 7.3: Word of Wisdom Word Circles" from the CD-ROM. Discuss the counsel given in D&C 89 for the specific items mentioned in this puzzle.

2. After reading the Word of Wisdom in D&C 89, have family members brainstorm some of the healthy items recommended for the human body. Make a healthy treat, such as a smoothie or a fruit and yogurt parfait, using some of the items family members mention.

3. Before reading the lesson, discuss how to feed and take care of a pet or houseplant. Make a list of what foods and liquids are needed to keep the animal or plant healthy. Discuss how it would not be a good idea, for example, to feed a dog chocolate or to water a plant with rubbing alcohol. Compare the guidelines for caring for the pet or plant to the counsel Heavenly Father has given us to care for our bodies.

Additional Resources:

1. Sugardoodle.net has a short article explaining how the Word of Wisdom came about (look for it under the educational lesson plans for the Word of Wisdom).

2. "Good Choices" is a color-by-number coloring page printed in the October 2005 *Friend*. It shows what types of foods are recommended in the Word of Wisdom.

George Albert Smith

CHAPTER EIGHT
GEORGE ALBERT SMITH

Introduction (Moroni 7:46)

Born on April 4, 1870, in Salt Lake City, George Albert Smith was a member of a distinguished LDS family. Both his father, John Henry Smith, and grandfather, George A. Smith, had served as counselors to Church presidents. In his youth he spent much time in the presence of Church leaders, later marrying Lucy Emily Woodruff, the granddaughter of President Wilford Woodruff. He was called at the age of thirty-three to the Quorum of the Twelve Apostles, beginning a long career of service in the Church despite fragile health and poor eyesight. He was a strong proponent of the Boy Scouts and served many years with the youth of the Church. George Albert Smith became president of the Church on May 21, 1945, a few weeks following World War II's V-E Day. He is well known for organizing the Church's massive welfare relief to Europe in the early years of his administration. President Smith lived a personal creed that he would be "a friend to the friendless" and strived to reach out to those in need.[65] After only six years as President, George A. Smith died in Salt Lake City on his eighty-first birthday in 1951.

---

[65] *Improvement Era*, March 1932, 295.

George Albert Smith's Testimony of Jesus Christ

"I have been buoyed up and, as it were, lifted out of myself and given power not my own to teach the glorious truths proclaimed by the Redeemer of the world. I have not seen Him face to face but have enjoyed the companionship of His Spirit and felt His presence in a way not to be mistaken. I know that my Redeemer lives and gladly yield my humble efforts to establish His teachings. The philosophies of men can never take the place of truth as revealed to us by the Eternal Father. Individual happiness and world-wide peace will not be permanent until those who dwell in the earth accept the Gospel and conform their lives to its precepts. It is the power of God unto salvation to all who believe and obey."[66]

Important Dates and Events in the Life of George Albert Smith

Birth—April 4, 1870, in Salt Lake City, Utah

Parents—Sarah Farr Smith and John Henry

Baptism—June 6, 1878 (age 8)

Mission—Southern States (1892–1894)

Marriage—May 25, 1892, to Lucy Emily Woodruff

Children—3

Called as an Apostle—October 8, 1903 (age 33)

Ordained Prophet—May 21, 1945 (age 75)

Years as Prophet—5 years, 10 months

Death—April 4, 1951, in Salt Lake City, Utah

---

[66] Forace Green, *Testimonies of Our Leaders* (Salt Lake City: Bookcraft, 1958), 53.

Lesson 1: Love Thy Neighbor

Purpose: To teach family members the importance of showing love and charity through small acts of kindness

Gospel Principles: Service, charity, kindness

Scripture: Matt. 25:40

Music: "Have I Done Any Good" (*Hymns*, no. 223), "When We're Helping We're Happy" (CS, 198)

Lesson: President Smith strived to exemplify Christ-like qualities in all facets of his personal life. He truly believed all are children of God and was happiest when he was in the service of others. There are many accounts of his helping the poor or visiting the sick. For example, once he arrived at home in winter without his coat. His wife, noticing he was chilled and shivering, asked him why he did not wear his coat, only to learn he had given it to a man in need. Another time, without being asked, he stopped by the home of Ezra Taft Benson to provide a blessing to an ill child in the absence of their father. Knowing how busy President Smith was, Elder Benson and his family were greatly touched by this act of kindness. George Albert Smith testified, "Do not forget no matter how much you may give in money, no matter how you may desire the things of this world to make yourselves happy, your happiness will be in proportion to your charity and to your kindness and to your love of those with whom you associate here on earth. Our Heavenly Father has said in very plain terms that he who says he loves God and does not love his brother is not truthful."[67]

---

[67] *Relief Society Magazine*, December 1932, 709.

Activities:

1. Print a copy of "Activity Page 8.1: George Albert Smith's Personal Creed Word Find" from the CD-ROM. After completing the word find, discuss some of the points in President Smith's personal creed. What might family members include if they were to write their own list of principles for living?

2. Tell family members how important it is to learn to treat others with love and kindness, just as George Albert Smith did. Role-play either the story of the Good Samaritan or modern-day opportunities to act with love and kindness in situations where it may not be so easy (such as times when children may argue with siblings, need to share, or are treated unkindly at school).

Additional Resources:

1. The September 2007 *Friend* has a coloring page of the Good Samaritan (page 41); picture 06048 090 in the Gospel Art Book also illustrates the story of the Good Samaritan.

2. "Serving Like Christ" is a word find game in the April 2009 *Friend* (page 43).

3. The Mormon Messages channel, which is available to watch online at www.lds.org, has produced a 2:29-minute video, *Have I Done Any Good in the World Today?* This short film features the words of Thomas S. Monson encouraging all to give service to others.

4. Refer to vineyard.lds.org to find volunteer service opportunities in the Church. This site notes, "The opportunities found here are comprised of hundreds of thousands of very small tasks. Collaborating as a group to complete these tasks, we can help further the work of the Church."

Lesson 2: Serving the Downtrodden

Purpose: To help family members develop an appreciation for showing love and kindness through humanitarian assistance

Gospel Principles: Humanitarian aid, service, welfare

Scripture: Ps. 82:3–5

Music: "Because I Have Been Given Much" (*Hymns*, no. 219), "'Give,' Said the Little Stream" (CS, 236)

Lesson:

George Albert Smith lived through a great deal of international turmoil, including two world wars and the Great Depression. Within a month following V-E Day President Heber J. Grant died, and George Albert Smith was sustained as president and prophet of the Church. One of his first and foremost concerns at the time was reaching out to those in Europe who were suffering in the aftermath of the war. In November 1945, President Smith paid a visit to Harry S. Truman, then president of the United States, to inquire about the possibility of sending humanitarian aid to Europe. President Smith described the visit as follows:

"When I called on him, he received me very graciously—I had met him before—and I said: 'I have just come to ascertain from you, Mr. President, what your attitude will be if the Latter-day Saints are prepared to ship food and clothing and bedding to Europe.'

"He smiled and looked at me, and said: 'Well, what do you want to ship it over there for? Their money isn't any good.'

"I said: 'We don't want their money.' He looked at me and asked: 'You don't mean you are going to give it to them?'

"I said: 'Of course, we would give it to them. They are our brothers and sisters and are in distress. God has blessed us with a surplus, and we will be glad to send it if we can have the co-operation of the government.'

"He said: 'You are on the right track' and added, 'we will be glad to help you in any way we can.'

"I have thought of that a good many times. After we had sat there a moment or two, he said again: 'How long will it take you to get this ready?'

"I said, 'It's all ready.'

"The government you remember had been destroying food and refusing to plant grain during the war, so I said to him:

"'Mr. President, while the administration at Washington were advising the destroying of food, we were building elevators and filling them with grain, and increasing our flocks and our herds, and now what we need is the cars and the ships in order to send considerable food, clothing and bedding to the people of Europe who are in distress. We have an organization in the Church that has over two thousand homemade quilts ready.'"[68]

The end result was that many Europeans received food, blankets, and other supplies before winter. As fast as the supplies could be loaded, they were delivered to relieve the people.

Activities:

1. Print a copy of "Activity Page 8.2: George Albert Smith Meets with President Truman" from the CD-ROM. Have

---

[68] George Albert Smith, *Conference Report*, October 1947, 5–6.

family members complete the dot-to-dot and color the picture while telling the story in the lesson.

2. Watch a video on www.lds.org/service/humanitarian about those who have benefited from humanitarian service projects. There are several videos posted here, each about 3:30 minutes long. Ask family members if it is important to give service to those we do not know or who live far away. Explain that the principles of humanitarian aid are based in those taught by the Savior and Joseph Smith, namely, "to feed the hungry, to clothe the naked, to provide for the widow, to dry up the tear of the orphan, to comfort the afflicted, whether in this church, or in any other, or in no church at all."[69]

3. Gather essential items for humanitarian donations; guidelines and suggested items are listed on the same website as the videos (see above).

Additional Resources:

1. President Dieter F. Uchtdorf, second counselor in the First Presidency, gave an applicable general conference address, "You Are My Hands," in April 2010.

2. In her *New Era* article "We Are His Hands" (July 2010), Sally Johnson Odekirk provides a list of humanitarian aid ideas for youth.

3. The Red Cross website has a "Giving and Getting Involved" section that may prove helpful in finding opportunities to serve.

---

[69] Joseph Smith, *Times and Seasons*, 15 March 1842, 732.

Lesson 3: Finding Peace in the World

Purpose: To help family members learn that inner peace can be found, despite the tumultuous world in which we live

Gospel Principles: Peace, faith, repentance, obedience

Scripture: D&C 59:23

Music: "Where Can I Turn For Peace" (*Hymns*, no. 129), "Keep the Commandments" (CS, 146)

Lesson:

Because of the war and economic uncertainty that persisted through much of George Albert Smith's life, he often spoke about finding inner peace during troubled times. He firmly believed that happiness and peace in this life was possible only if individuals repented, obeyed the commandments, and exercised faith in the Savior. In the general conference of October 1915, Elder George Albert Smith said:

"Though the world may be filled with distress, and the heavens gather blackness, and the vivid lightnings flash, and the earth quake from center to circumference, if we know that God lives, and our lives are righteous, we will be happy, there will be peace unspeakable because we know our Father approves of our lives."[70]

And in the April 1934 conference he noted:

"There is much confusion in the world and there seems to be no way to remove it except by the power of our Heavenly Father. The wisdom of the world is failing, the scripture is fulfilled, and today the wisest of all men are seeking, by means of legislation, to bring about a better condition and

---

[70] *Conference Report*, October 1915.

a more wholesome life among the human family. They may strive in that way, but unless men have faith in God, unless they understand the purpose of life, they will not go very far. The people of the world must repent of their sins before the Lord can give to them the peace and happiness desired. No other plan will succeed."[71]

Activities:

1. Print a copy of "Activity Page 8.3: Five in a Row" from the CD-ROM. Play several rounds of this game before giving the lesson. Compare the difficulty of this game to being able to find peace in real life. Remind family members that President Smith taught that we will have inner peace only if we repent and obey the commandments.

2. As a family, take time to learn the song "Peace is a Feeling," written by Clive Romney and published in the *Friend*.[72] Encourage family members to sing this song when they feel upset or worried.

Additional Resources:

1. A thorough study of peace is addressed on the "Gospel Study" page on www.lds.org; it includes quotes, scriptures, and a list of articles on the subject.

2. An April 2004 *Liahona* article answers the question, "How can I feel peace with so many frightening things happening in the world and even in my own school?"[73]

---

[71] *Conference Report*, April 1934, 27.
[72] Clive Romney, "Peace Is a Feeling," *Friend*, October 1994, 46.
[73] "Questions and Answers," *Liahona*, April 2004, 44.

David O. McKay

CHAPTER NINE
DAVID O. MCKAY

Introduction (John 21:15)

One of the longest-serving prophets of the latter days is President David O. McKay. Sustained as prophet in April 1951, President McKay led the Church for more than eighteen years. Born in the summer of 1873, David O. McKay grew up in Huntsville, Utah, on his parents' farm. Later, he studied at the Weber Stake Academy and the University of Utah with the aim of becoming a teacher; he is the first prophet in the latter days who earned a college degree. After graduating from college and serving a mission, he married Emma Ray Riggs and embarked on his career in education. As a member of the Weber Stake Sunday School presidency, he helped to greatly improve teaching and drew the notice of leaders. By age thirty-two he was called as an apostle. Helping the Church transition toward becoming a worldwide organization, he established the first stakes outside the United States and selected Switzerland as the location of the first temple across the Atlantic. After nearly sixty-five years as a Church leader, David O. McKay died on January 18, 1970, in Salt Lake City.

David O. McKay's Testimony of Jesus Christ

"'How can we know the way?' asked Thomas, as he sat with his fellow apostles and their Lord at the table after the supper on the memorable night of the betrayal; and Christ's divine answer was: 'I am the Way, the Truth, and the Life . . . .' (John 14:5–6.) And so He is! He is the source of our comfort, the inspiration of our life, the author of our salvation. If we want to know our relationship to God, we go to Jesus Christ. If we would know the truth of the immortality of the soul, we have it exemplified in the Savior's resurrection."[74]

Important Dates and Events in the Life of David O. McKay

Birth—September 8, 1873, in Huntsville, Utah

Parents—Jennette Evans and David McKay

Baptism—September 8, 1881 (age 8)

Mission—Great Britain (1897–1899)

Marriage—January 2, 1901, to Emma Ray Riggs

Children—7

Called as an Apostle—April 9, 1906 (age 32)

Ordained Prophet—April 9, 1951 (age 77)

Years as Prophet—18 years, 9 months

Death—January 18, 1970, in Salt Lake City, Utah

---

[74] *Conference Report*, April 1968, 6–7.

Lesson 1: Value of Family Life

Purpose: To help family members understand the importance of family life in learning to live gospel principles

Gospel Principles: Family, marriage, teaching

Scripture: Mosiah 4:14–15

Music: "Love at Home" (*Hymns*, no. 294), "Love is Spoken Here" (CS, 190)

Lesson:

President McKay once said, "The older I grow the more grateful I am for my parents, for how they lived the gospel in that old country home. . . . Both father and mother lived the gospel."[75] He firmly believed that the family was one of life's greatest blessings and, if patterned after righteousness, would enable children to learn how to live the gospel and to gain a personal testimony of their own. In his own youth, David O. McKay was well taught by his parents to live the gospel. They regularly had family prayer and scripture study. And when David's father left to serve a mission, his mother made sure the family faithfully continued these practices. On one occasion, David recalled being frightened by a storm in the night. Despite his fear, he knelt to pray for the safety of his home and family. Soon after he heard a voice say, "Don't be afraid; nothing will hurt you."[76] Later in his life President McKay and his wife, Emma Ray, taught their own children the gospel through faithful living in the home. He is also well known for quoting James McCulloch's words, "No other success can compensate for failure in the home."[77]

---

[75] *Conference Report*, October 1960, 85–86.
[76] Kellene Ricks, "David Oman McKay," *Friend*, September 1989, 40.
[77] *Conference Report*, April 1964, 5.

Activities:

1. Print a copy of "Activity Page 9.1: Happiness in the Home Hidden Maze" from the CD-ROM. After completing the maze, discuss how important it is to follow David O. McKay's advice to make home life one of happiness and joy.

2. After reading the lesson, discuss as a family some ways to improve gospel living in your home. Review President McKay's ten points for having a happy home (listed below). Set a goal and determine a reward for reaching it within a specific time period.

1. Ever keep in mind that you begin to lay the foundation of a happy home in your pre-marital lives. While in courtship you should learn to be loyal and true to your future husband or wife. Keep yourselves clean and pure. Cherish the highest ideals of chastity and purity. Do not be deceived.

2. Choose your mate by judgment and inspiration, as well as by physical attraction. Intellect and breeding are vital and important in the human family.

3. Approach marriage with the lofty view it merits. Marriage is ordained of God. It is not something to be entered into lightly or to be dissolved at the first difficulty that arises.

4. Remember that the noblest purpose of marriage is procreation. Home is children's natural nursery. Happiness in the home is enhanced by having children at the fireside.

5. Let the spirit of reverence pervade the home. Have your home such that if the Savior called unexpectedly He could be invited to stay and not feel out of His element. Pray in the home.

6. Let husband or wife never speak in loud tones to each other.

7. Learn the value of self-control. We are never sorry for the word unspoken. Lack of self-control is the greatest source of unhappiness in the home. Children should be taught self-control, self-respect, and respect for others.

8. Fasten home ties by continued companionship. Companionship fosters love. Do everything to cement love for all eternity.

9. Make accessible to children proper literature and music.

10. By example and precept, encourage participation in Church activity. This is fundamental in developing a true character. Church activity should be led, not directed, by parents.[78]

Additional Resources:

1. An illustrated version of the story of David O. McKay praying during the storm was published in the September 1989 *Friend* (see page 40).

2. An informative biographical video on the life of David O. McKay has been posted on YouTube (see Mormon History: LDS [Mormon] Prophet David O. McKay 1/2 posted on channel LDS9999).

---

[78] *The Presidents of the Church*, 155–156.

Lesson 2: The Importance of Education

Purpose: To help family members understand the important role of education throughout this life

Gospel Principles: Education, scripture study, learning

Scripture: D&C 88:118

Music: "Truth Eternal" (Hymns, no. 4), "Seek the Lord Early" (CS, 108)

Lesson:

President David O. McKay was raised on a farm but knew early in his life that he did not want to be a farmer. He loved to learn and spent as much time as he could reading and studying, and he was blessed to be able to attend college after his mother received some money in an inheritance. While attending the University of Utah he played football, was involved in student government, and studied so hard he was able to graduate as valedictorian. A year after he became president of the Church, President McKay spoke to the student body at Brigham Young University about the importance of getting a college education: "University life is essentially an exercise in thinking, preparing and living. . . . The aim of education is to develop resources in the child that will contribute to his well-being as long as life endures; to develop power of self-mastery that he may never be a slave to indulgence or other weaknesses, . . . one who can face life with courage, meet disaster with fortitude, and face death without fear."[79]

---

[79] David O. McKay, with an introduction by President Ernest L. Wilkinson, "Address to the BYU Student Body," Wednesday, October 8, 1952.

Activities:

1. Print a copy of "Activity Page 9.2: Seek Learning" from the CD-ROM. Explain to children what studies each of the college majors include. Ask each family member to name the major that sounds the most interesting to him or her.

2. Explore the required education for a specific skill or career in which individual family members have expressed interest. Discuss what they can do now to prepare for this training (some examples might include study hard in school, get good grades, get involved in appropriate extracurricular activities, and so on).

3. Discuss the following quote by President Henry B. Eyring, including how one can learn continually to develop his or her talents: "The Lord and His Church have always encouraged education to increase our ability to serve Him and our Heavenly Father's children. For each of us, whatever our talents, He has service for us to give. And to do it well always involves learning, not once or for a limited time, but continually."[80]

Additional Resources:

1. Review the Church's education website at www.besmart.com to learn more about college preparation.

2. *The Encyclopedia of Mormonism* contains two informative entries regarding education ("Attitudes toward Education" and "Educational Attainment").

---

[80] From a talk given on the 75th anniversary of the Institute of Religion program at a Church Educational System fireside in Moscow, Idaho, on May 6, 2001.

Lesson 3: Act Well Thy Part

Purpose: To encourage family members to commit to do their best in each and every opportunity and calling the Lord may provide

Gospel Principles: Obedience, service, discipleship

Scripture: D&C 43:9–10

Music: "I'll Go Where You Want Me to Go" (*Hymns*, no. 270), "I Will Be Valiant" (CS, 162)

Lesson:

President David O. McKay was blessed to be called to serve a mission in Scotland, where his father's family originated. While serving in Stirling, Scotland, Elder McKay was homesick and faced some difficult challenges. However, an important experience happened that influenced his outlook for the rest of his life. He and his companion saw a carved inscription in an arch over a doorway that read, "What e'er thou art, act well thy part." Later, President McKay said this message seemed to come to him, "not only in stone, but as if it came from One in whose service we were engaged." He knew after reading the carving that it was his duty to perform his service as a missionary with full commitment and dedication, and he promised the Lord he would do so. In 1955 President McKay had the opportunity to revisit Stirling and went again to see this inscription, sharing his experience with those who traveled with him.[81]

---

[81] "Lesson 29: David O. McKay—Worldwide Ambassador of God," *The Presidents of the Church: Teacher's Manual* (1996), 147–148.

Activities:

1. Print a copy of "Activity Page 9.3: The McKay Stone" from the CD-ROM. Have family members color the McKay Stone coloring page. After reading President McKay's experience, have family members select an area in their life in which they can strive to "act well thy part." Write this commitment at the bottom of the coloring page and place the page in a visible location to serve as a reminder.

2. The original McKay Stone is now on display in the Museum of Church History and Art in Salt Lake City. Additionally, a replica of the McKay Stone is near the entrance of the Missionary Training Center in Provo, Utah. If convenient, take the family to visit one of these locations.

Additional Resources:

1. The missionary journals of President David O. McKay have been published in the book *What E'er Thou Art Act Well Thy Part: The Missionary Journals of David O. McKay* (Freethinker Press, 1999).

2. BYUtv.org has a ninety-minute biographical program, *David O. McKay: Act Well Thy Part*, available for viewing on the Internet. The production includes interviews with President McKay's children, various historians, and President Thomas S. Monson.

3. The January 1995 *New Era* Mormon Ad poster focuses on the phrase "Act Well Thy Part."

Joseph Fielding Smith

CHAPTER TEN
JOSEPH FIELDING SMITH

Introduction (John 21:15)

As grandson of patriarch Hyrum Smith and son of President Joseph F. Smith (sixth president of the Church), Joseph Fielding Smith was blessed with a particularly rich heritage. Born July 19, 1876, in Salt Lake City, Joseph Fielding showed early in his life a tendency toward studiousness and scholarship. He served a mission in England a year after marrying Louie Emily Shurtliff. Later he found employment in the Church historian's office. After being called as an apostle at age thirty-three, President Smith worked diligently to teach the correct doctrines of the Church and became a prolific writer of books and articles. He served as president of the Quorum of the Twelve Apostles for the entire tenure of President David O. McKay and became prophet in 1970 at age ninety-three. He served as prophet for approximately two and a half years, during which time missionary work expanded, two temples were dedicated, and the Church magazines were consolidated.

Joseph Fielding Smith's Testimony of Jesus Christ

"Do you think it will ever be possible for any one of us, no matter how hard we labor, or even if we should suffer martyrdom, to pay our Father and Jesus Christ for the blessings we have received from them? The great love, with its accompanying blessings, extended to us through the crucifixion, suffering, and resurrection of Jesus Christ is beyond our mortal comprehension. We could never repay. We have been bought with a price beyond computation—not with gold or silver or precious stones, 'but with the precious blood of Christ, as of a lamb without blemish, and without spot' (1 Peter 1:19)."[82]

Important Dates and Events in the Life of Joseph Fielding Smith

Birth—July 19, 1876, in Salt Lake City, Utah

Parents—Julina Lambson and Joseph F. Smith

Baptism—July 19, 1884 (age 8)

Mission—England (1899–1901)

Marriage—April 26, 1898, to Louie Emily Shurtliff (first wife)

Children—11

Called as an Apostle—April 7, 1910 (age 33)

Ordained Prophet—January 23, 1970 (age 93)

Years as Prophet—2 years, 5 months

Death—July 2, 1972, in Salt Lake City, Utah

---

[82] *Conference Report*, April 1966, 102.

Lesson 1: Effective Scripture Study

Purpose: To help family members learn the basic principles of successful scripture study habits

Gospel Principles: Scripture study, gospel principles, knowledge

Scripture: Mosiah 4:14–15

Music: "The Iron Rod" (*Hymns*, no. 274), "Seek the Lord Early" (CS, 108)

Lesson:

Joseph Fielding Smith is considered one of the Church's greatest gospel scholars. From his youth he exhibited a love of reading and study; he finished the Book of Mormon twice before the age of ten. In the April 1930 general conference, President Smith stated, "From my earliest recollection, from the time I first could read, I have received more pleasure and greater satisfaction out of the study of the scriptures, and reading of the Lord Jesus Christ, and of the Prophet Joseph Smith, and the work that has been accomplished for the salvation of men, than from anything else in all the world."[83]

Joseph Fielding McConkie, grandson of Joseph Fielding Smith and former professor of ancient scripture at Brigham Young University, has stated that the secret to his grandfather's effective scripture study habits was that he was *consistent* and *intense* in his study. Brother McConkie also shared the following seven tips for studying the scriptures successfully:

Know that it takes the spirit of revelation to understand revelation.

---

[83] *Conference Report*, April 1930, 91.

Remember that all gospel principles are absolute; from eternity to eternity they are the same.

"Seek learning, even by study and also by faith."

Keep things in context.

Remember that there is a balance to maintain between gospel principles.

Freely seek help from sources that may exceed your knowledge—use commentaries and your common sense.

Enhance your scripture study by applying, or likening, the scriptures unto yourselves.[84]

Activities:

1. Print a copy of "Activity Page 10.1: Scripture Study Scripture Chase" from the CD-ROM. Cut out each of the scriptures and place them in a container. Have a family member draw one scripture out at a time and read it aloud. Race to see who can find the verse first in their scriptures.

2. Make a scripture study chart, either for the family as a whole or for individual family members. Encourage family members to read their scriptures with consistency and intensity, as did President Smith. Set a goal to complete the scripture reading chart. Don't forget a reward!

---

[84] Joseph Fielding McConkie, "The 'How' of Scriptural Study," in *By Study and By Faith: Selections from the* Religious Educator, ed. Richard Neitzel Holzapfel and Kent P. Jackson (Provo, UT: Religious Studies Center, Brigham Young University, 2009), 51–67.

Additional Resources:

1. The *Church News* article, "How to Make Family Scripture Study Fun, Interesting," gives some practical and easy ideas for improving scripture study in families of all types (published Saturday, June 11, 1994).

2. The *Marriage and Family Relations* instructor's manual has a lesson (#16) that touches on family scripture study and family prayer. This manual is available online at www. lds.org and should also be available in the library of most meetinghouses.

3. The website www.scriptures4kids.com provides a variety of scripture study opportunities for LDS kids of all ages. There are also scripture-based games, reading charts, songs, challenges, and other resources available on this site.

Lesson 2: Preparing for the Second Coming

Purpose: To help family members recognize the signs of the Second Coming of the Savior

Gospel Principles: Second Coming, Jesus Christ, last days

Scripture: D&C 64:23–24

Music: "Come, Ye Children of the Lord" (*Hymns*, no. 58), "I Wonder When He Comes Again" (CS, 82)

Lesson:

One of the topics Joseph Fielding Smith often spoke on is that of the Second Coming of the Savior. His book, *The Signs of the Times* (1942), was published after numerous requests for copies of lectures he had given on the last days.

The scriptures prophesy Jesus Christ will return to the earth again to usher in the Millennium. President Smith taught that the Second Coming of Christ will come in the day of wickedness, when the earth is ripe in iniquity and prepared for the cleansing. During the Second Coming, all the wicked will be as stubble and will be consumed. President Smith wrote:

> I do not know when he is going to come. No man knows. Even the angels of heaven are in the dark in regard to that great truth. [See Matthew 24:36–37.] But this I know, that the signs that have been pointed out are here. The earth is full of calamity, of trouble. The hearts of men are failing them. We see the signs as we see the fig tree putting forth her leaves; and knowing this time is near, it behooves me and it behooves you, and all men upon the face of the earth, to pay heed to the words of Christ, to his

apostles and watch, for we know not the day nor the hour. But I tell you this, it shall come as a thief in the night, when many of us will not be ready for it.[85]

Although the Second Coming will be a time of great wickedness, President Smith also encouraged the Saints, stating that obedience to gospel principles will help to protect the righteous in the last days. By being obedient and watching for the signs, the Saints can find peace and joy despite the wickedness of the world.

Activities:

1. Print a copy of "Activity Page 10.2: Signs of the Times" from the CD-ROM. Look up each of the scriptures to fill in the blanks describing the signs of the Second Coming.

2. Give each individual a pair of scissors, a blank piece of paper, and a glue stick. Using magazines and newspapers, have family members cut out headlines and photos to make a collage illustrating the signs of the times about which President Joseph Fielding Smith taught.

Additional Resources:

1. The December 1999 *Friend* magazine has flannel board cutouts that can be used to teach about the Second Coming (see page 10). These could also be used as a coloring page activity during family home evening.

2. There are numerous lessons published in Church manuals on the Second Coming that could be used as supplementary

---

[85] Joseph Fielding Smith with Bruce R. McConkie, ed., *Doctrines of Salvation: Sermons and Writings of Joseph Fielding Smith* (Salt Lake City: Bookcraft, 1992), 3:52–53.

material. Three of these lessons are the New Testament Gospel Doctrine lesson 21, Gospel Principles chapters 43 or 44, and Primary 7 New Testament lesson 46.

3. The Gospel Art Kit 238 is an illustration of the Second Coming.

Lesson 3: Fatherhood

Purpose: To help family members recognize the importance of fathers in teaching and guiding children

Gospel Principles: Fatherhood, family, heritage

Scripture: 1 Ne. 1:1

Music: "O My Father" (*Hymns*, no. 292), "Daddy's Homecoming" (CS, 210)

Lesson:

As the son of Joseph F. Smith (sixth president of the Church) and grandson of Hyrum Smith (brother of the Prophet Joseph Smith), Joseph Fielding Smith came from a rich patriarchal heritage. This legacy greatly influenced and shaped him throughout his life. For example, his tendency toward scholarship was fueled by tutoring from his father. Joseph Fielding had many memories of being taught the gospel at his father's knee; later in his life, he stated, "I have a great love for my father. It was marvelous how the words of living light and fire flowed from him." Because of this tenderness for his father, he was all the more diligent in living the gospel, often asking himself in the face of temptation, "What would my father think of that?"

In addition to having affection for his own father, grandfather, and grand-uncle, Joseph Fielding Smith was a devoted father himself. He was always called "father" by his children and "granddaddy" by his grandchildren. He loved to spend time with his family and taught his children the gospel during breakfast or in other family gatherings. Family members and Church leaders alike have paid homage to Joseph Fielding Smith for his devotion to family, both as a husband and father. Harold B. Lee, who succeeded President Smith as the prophet, later commented, "Truly, the greatest monument to him is the great posterity which he has given the world."[86]

Activities:

1. Print a copy of "Activity Page 10.3: Color by Numbers for Fathers" from the CD-ROM. Have a father, grandfather, or other influential male answer the quiz. Then color the picture according to the colors for each quiz answer.

2. Gather pictures of Joseph Smith Sr., Lucy Mack Smith, Joseph Smith Jr., Hyrum Smith, Mary Fielding, Joseph F. Smith, and Julina Lambson. Use these pictures to create a visual family tree as part of the lesson. Discuss the various contributions that Joseph Fielding Smith's family members made in his life and to the restored gospel on the earth.

3. Spend time making some thank-you pictures or notes for the fathers, grandfathers, or uncles who have been a blessing to your family.

Additional Resources:

1. Susan Evans McCloud, niece of President Joseph Fielding Smith, published two articles in the Deseret News describing personal experiences she had with her uncle. These articles share personal accounts that speak to President Smith and his love for family (published in March 2011).

2. Read more about the childhood of President Joseph Fielding Smith in the Presidents of the Church institute manual (Chapter 10).

---

[86] Amelia S. McConkie and Mark L. McConkie, "Smith, Joseph Fielding," Encyclopedia of Mormonism: Church History (New York: MacMillan Publishing, 1992), 531–532.

3. An illustrated story of Joseph Fielding Smith and his father, Joseph F. Smith, was published in the *Friend* magazine in October 1989 ("Joseph Fielding Smith," written by Kellene Ricks).

Harold B. Lee

CHAPTER ELEVEN
HAROLD B. LEE

Introduction (Matt. 11:28–30)

The eleventh president of the Church, Harold B. Lee, was prophet for seventeen months, the shortest tenure as president to date. Born in Clifton, Idaho, in 1899, Lee received a good education in his youth, both scholastically and musically. He served a mission in the Western States Mission, spending much of his time in the Denver, Colorado, area. Called as a stake president during the darkest days of the Depression, President Lee became well known for the self-help relief program he implemented for the welfare of those in his care. Later, as a member of the Quorum of the Twelve Apostles, he continued his work with the Church's Welfare Program. Additionally, President Lee helped oversee the correlation effort of teaching and training in Church auxiliaries worldwide. President Harold B. Lee succeeded Joseph Fielding Smith as prophet in 1972. Church members were surprised and saddened when he passed away suddenly in late 1973 at age seventy-four.[87]

---

[87] Brent L. Goates, "Lee, Harold B.," *Selections from the Encyclopedia of Mormonism: Church History* (Salt Lake City: Deseret Book Company), 297.

Harold B. Lee's Testimony of Jesus Christ

Soon after being called as an apostle, Elder Lee had a sacred experience: "During the days which followed, I locked myself in one of the rooms over in the Church Office Building, and there I read the story of the life of the Savior. As I read the events of His life, and particularly the events leading up to and of the crucifixion, and then of the resurrection, I discovered that something was happening to me. I was not just reading a story; it seemed actually as though I was living the events; and I was reading them with a reality the like of which I had never before experienced." Later, he testified of the Savior saying, "I, too, know that these things are true, that Jesus died and was resurrected for the sins of the world." He spoke with a full heart, because he had come to know that week, "with a certainty which I never before had known."[88]

Important Dates and Events in the Life of Harold B. Lee

Birth—March 28, 1899, in Clifton, Idaho

Parents—Louisa Bingham and Samuel Marion Lee

Baptism—June 9, 1907 (age 8)

Mission—Western States Mission (1920–1922)

Marriage—November 14, 1923, to Fern Lucinda Tanner

Children—2

Called as an Apostle—April 10, 1941 (age 42)

Ordained Prophet—July 7, 1972 (age 73)

Years as Prophet—1 year, 5 months

Death—December 26, 1973, in Salt Lake City, Utah

[88] *Conference Report*, April 1952.

Lesson 1: Keep the Commandments

Purpose: To help family members learn the importance of keeping the commandments as a way to find safety and peace in this life

Gospel Principles: Righteous living, obedience, agency

Scripture: John 15:10

Music: "Choose the Right" (*Hymns*, no. 239), "Keep the Commandments" (*Hymns*, no. 303; CS, 146)

Lesson:

In July 1972, Harold B. Lee became the eleventh president of the Church. One hour after the announcement was made he met with newspaper and television reporters for a press conference. More than fifty reporters were there to ask President Lee questions; one of them asked if he had a message for Church members. President Lee responded by saying, "Keep the commandments of God. Therein will be the salvation of individuals and nations during these troublesome times. . . . The safety of the Church lies in the members keeping the commandments. There is nothing more important that I could say. As they keep the commandments, blessings will come."[89]

Barbara A. McConochie was so touched by President Lee's council she was inspired to write the Primary song, "Keep the Commandments." The words of the song are based on Harold B. Lee's response during the press conference.

Sister McConochie has said of her song, "Keeping the commandments is the anchor for our safety amidst the storm. True peace will come to each individual, family, and nation

---

[89] *Church News*, July 15, 1972, 3.

only as we learn obedience to the laws of our Heavenly Father."[90]

Activities:

1. Print a copy of "Activity Page 11.1: Blessings of Keeping the Commandments" from the CD-ROM.

2. After reading the above story about President Lee, memorize the song "Keep the Commandments" by using the Primary songbook (music also available on tape/CD, as well as online). Additionally, try to learn the sign language for the words of this song. A video of the signed song is available on www.lds.org.

3. Give each family member a piece of paper. Have family members write down or draw pictures of three commandments they feel they can keep. Use illustrations from Church magazines to help provide suggestions.

Additional Resources:

1. A coloring page about keeping the commandments was published in the April 1994 *Friend* magazine.

2. Numerous suggestions and flipchart ideas for teaching the song "Keep the Commandments" are available on www.sugardoodle.net under the Primary song index.

3. The book *Our Latter-day Hymns* by Karen Lynn Davidson (Salt Lake City: Deseret Book, 1988) tells the background and history of each of the hymns, including "Keep the Commandments." It also contains a brief biographical sketch on Barbara A. McConochie.

---

[90] Judy Edwards, "Sharing Time: Keep the Commandments," *Friend*, April 1994, 12.

Lesson 2: Be Loyal to the Royal within You

Purpose: To help family members learn the importance of living up to their personal potential and family heritage

Gospel Principles: Heritage, obedience, standards

Scripture: 1 Pet. 2:9

Music: "Behold, A Royal Army" (*Hymns*, 251), "Quickly I'll Obey" (CS, 197B)

Lesson:

In a speech given at Brigham Young University three months before he died, President Harold B. Lee taught: "May I just offer one or two more thoughts. One of our Latter-day Saint men during World War II was over in England. He had gone to an officer's club where they were holding a riotous kind of celebration. He noticed off to the side a young British officer who didn't seem to be enjoying himself at all. So he walked over to him and said, 'You don't seem to be enjoying this kind of a party.' And this young British officer straightened himself a few inches taller than he was before and replied, 'No, sir, I can't engage in this kind of a party, because, you see, I belong to the royal household of England.'

"As our Latter-day Saint boy walked away he said to himself, 'Neither can I, because I belong to the royal household of the kingdom of God.' Do you realize that, you young people? There are things that you cannot and must not do if you remember your heritage.

"I am reminded of the old court jester who was supposed to entertain his king with interesting stories and antics. He looked at the king who was lolling on his throne, a drunken, filthy rascal, doffed his cap and bells, and said with a mock gesture of obeisance, 'O king, be loyal to the royal within you.' And so I say to you young people today, remember your heritage, and be loyal to that royal lineage that you have as members of the church and kingdom of God on the earth."[91]

Activities:

1. Print a copy of "Activity Page 11.2: Be Loyal to the Royal within You" from the CD-ROM. Let family members color it during family home evening. Place a 4" x 6" photograph in the frame and display it in a prominent location to remind family members of this lesson.

2. Share the stories given above in the lesson then tell some personal family history stories to illustrate the royal lineage of your family. Discuss what actions would demonstrate being "loyal to the royal."

Additional Resources:

1. This lesson is based on a speech given by President Lee at Brigham Young University in 1973; read the entire speech on http://speeches.byu.edu.

2. The November 2004 *New Era* poster was based on the phrase "Be Loyal to the Royal Within You."

3. The manual *Teachings of the Presidents of the Church: Harold B. Lee* has a lesson covering this topic (see Chapter 10: Loving, Faithful Priesthood Service).

---

[91] BYU devotional address 11, September 1973.

Lesson 3: The Welfare Program

Purpose: To help family members understand the value and importance of the Church Welfare Program in assisting members in need

Gospel Principles: Welfare, preparedness, bishops

Scripture: D&C 51:13

Music: "Improve the Shining Moments" (*Hymns*, no. 226), "Our Bishop" (CS, 135)

Lesson:

Harold B. Lee first witnessed Church welfare work as a child; he watched his father, who served as a bishop in Idaho, run his own bishop's storehouse—although the stock came from his own home pantry. Young Harold would see his father leave to deliver provisions to those who were in need.[92]

In 1930 Harold B. Lee was called to serve as a stake president in Salt Lake City. The Depression was in full force and half of his stake members were unemployed. He felt a great need to minister to both the physical and spiritual needs of those in his care. He did so by establishing a welfare program to help members. As part of the program, he helped organize the Pioneer Stake bishop's storehouse in 1932. The storehouse provided members who were willing to work there with basic food necessities. This model of welfare assistance through bishop's storehouses was very successful and was later adopted by the Church as a whole. Seventy-five years later, the current Church Welfare Program is based on the same model developed by President Lee.[93]

---

[92] Breck England, "Harold B. Lee: Master Teacher," *Ensign*, January 2002, 14.

[93] Brent L. Goates, "Lee, Harold B.," *Selections from the Encyclopedia*

Activities:

1. Print a copy of "Activity Page 11.3: Welfare Square Don't Eat Pete" from the CD-ROM. After each turn, discuss the meaning of the square that was "Pete" and its relation to welfare.

2. With younger children, set up a pretend bishop's storehouse using toy food, empty food containers, or boxes of food items. Have a child pretend to be the bishop, delivering the food to other needy family members. Make a simple costume by dressing the "bishop" up in a tie and name card.

3. If possible, arrange to visit and/or volunteer at a local bishop's storehouse.

Additional Resources:

1. "Lessons Learned at the Bishop's Storehouse" is an *Ensign* article summarizing the experiences one sister had receiving assistance from the Welfare Program.[94]

2. The LDS999 channel on YouTube has two different videos of general authorities speaking in general conference about the Welfare program (President Gordon B. Hinckley and Joseph B. Wirthlin, both uploaded in June 2008). Also, the *St. Louis Post Dispatch* (STLPostDispatch channel) has posted a 1:18-minute YouTube video that shows volunteers at a bishop's storehouse and briefly explains the welfare work completed there.

---

of *Mormonism: Church History* (Salt Lake City: Deseret Book Company), 297.

[94] Jackie Witzel, "Lessons Learned at the Bishops' Storehouse," *Ensign*, December 2001, 53–55.

3. A cartoon based on the life of Harold B. Lee and his contribution to the Welfare Program of the Church was published in the *Friend* in December 2001.[95]

---

[95] "Harold B. Lee Shares Christmas," *Friend*, December 2001, 28–29.

Spencer W. Kimball

CHAPTER TWELVE
SPENCER W. KIMBALL

Introduction (Mosiah 3:17–18)

Two days before the beginning of 1974, Spencer W. Kimball was ordained as prophet. Due to a history of serious health issues, many felt he would not serve long as head of the Church. However, his almost twelve-year tenure proved to be extremely fruitful as the Church nearly doubled in size, growing into an international organization. Some attribute President Kimball's strong leadership skills to his humble and loving manner. As the grandson of Heber C. Kimball, Spencer W. Kimball was born in 1895 in Salt Lake City but grew up in Arizona's Gila Valley, where he was able to observe his father serve as a stake president. Spencer learned to work hard in his youth and held a variety of jobs, including working on a dairy farm, working in a bank, and running his own insurance company. He was called as an apostle in 1943 at age forty-eight. During his presidency, the number of operating temples doubled, the number of missionaries increased by 50 percent, and the priesthood was extended to all worthy male members. He died in Salt Lake City on November 5, 1985.[96]

---

[96] Edward L. Kimball, "Kimball, Spencer W.," *Encyclopedia of Mormonism: Church History* (New York: MacMillan Publishing, 1992), 272–279.

Spencer W. Kimball's Testimony of Jesus Christ

"Knowing full well that before long, in the natural course of
events, I must stand before the Lord and give an accounting
of my words, I now add my personal and solemn testimony
that God, the Eternal Father, and the risen Lord, Jesus Christ,
appeared to the boy Joseph Smith. I testify that the Book of
Mormon is a translation of an ancient record of nations who
once lived in this western hemisphere, where they prospered
and became mighty when they kept the commandments of
God, but who were largely destroyed through terrible civil
wars when they forgot God. This book bears testimony of
the living reality of the Lord Jesus Christ as the Savior and
Redeemer of mankind."[97]

Important Dates and Events in the Life of Spencer W. Kimball

Birth—March 28, 1895, in Salt Lake City, Utah

Parents—Olive Woolley and Andrew Kimball

Baptism—March 28, 1903 (age 8)

Mission—Central States Mission (1914–1916)

Marriage—November 16, 1917, to Camilla Eyring

Children—4

Called as an Apostle—October 7, 1943 (age 48)

Ordained Prophet—December 30, 1973 (age 78)

Years as Prophet—11 years, 10 months

Death—November 5, 1985, in Salt Lake City, Utah

[97] "Remarks and Dedication of the Fayette, New York, Buildings,"
Ensign, May 1980, 54.

Lesson 1: Lengthen Your Stride

Purpose: To help family members have the desire to live the gospel more fully in their day-to-day lives

Gospel Principles: Stewardship, obedience, valiance

Scripture: D&C 104:11–13

Music: "Put Your Shoulder to the Wheel" (*Hymns*, no. 252), "I Will Be Valiant" (*CS*, 162)

Lesson:

President Kimball challenged the Saints several times to "lengthen your stride." In a 1975 *Ensign* article he wrote, "We have the gospel of Jesus Christ, the gospel of peace, the gospel of joy. We have truths that can make any person better and more fulfilled, any marriage happier and sweeter, any home more heavenly. . . . Yes, it is to ourselves, our homes, our quorums, our classes, our Church assignments that we must carry more energetically those things that we have received. . . . We must lengthen our stride and must do it now."[98]

How does one lengthen his stride? By trying to do a little bit more, day by day, on a consistent basis. President Kimball himself was a good example of this; he always tried to do just a little bit better and set goals for himself. His personal motto was "Do it!" President Kimball told of a personal experience he had as a teen learning the value of this concept: "Let me tell you of one of the goals that I made when I was still but a lad. When I heard a Church leader from Salt Lake City tell us at conference that we should read the scriptures, and I recognized that I had never read the Bible, that very night at

---

[98] Spencer W. Kimball, "Always a Convert Church: Some Lessons to Learn and Apply This Year," *Ensign*, September 1975, 2.

the conclusion of that very sermon I walked to my home a block away and climbed up in my little attic room in the top of the house and lighted a little coal-oil lamp that was on the little table, and I read the first chapters of Genesis. A year later I closed the Bible, having read every chapter in the big and glorious book."[99]

Activities:

1. Print a copy of "Activity Page 12.1: Lengthen Your Stride Coloring Page" from the CD-ROM. Let family members color as the lesson is given. Ask family members to write on the coloring page one way in which they will try to live the gospel more fully during the upcoming week.

2. Use masking tape to create a line on the floor. Have family members stand with their toes on the line. Then have each individual take one step forward. Using an additional piece of tape, mark where the back of each person's heel lands. Tell family members this is the length of their stride. Have them stand behind the starting line once more and take another step that is a little longer—lengthening their stride. Explain that "lengthening your stride" in living the gospel means that each individual tries harder to fulfill responsibilities and duties "more energetically."

Additional Resources:

1. President Kimball's son, Edward, is the author of the book *Lengthen Your Stride: The Presidency of Spencer W. Kimball* (Salt Lake City: Shadow Mountain, 2005), which focuses exclusively on President Kimball's ministry as president of the Church and which discusses a number of landmark events during his tenure.

---

[99] Spencer W. Kimball, "Planning for a Full and Abundant Life," *Ensign*, May 1974, 86.

2. *The Presidents of the Church* teacher's manual (1996) has a chapter on "Lengthen Your Stride" and President Kimball (Chapter 39). The student manual of *The Presidents of the Church* is available online at www.ldsces.org and has a biographical chapter on the life of Spencer W. Kimball (Chapter 12).

3. A crossword puzzle of words taken from the life of President Kimball was published in the September 2001 *Friend* magazine (pages 26–27).

Lesson 2: Overcoming Personal Trials

Purpose: To help family members understand that trials help individuals grow and make it possible to draw closer to the Lord

Gospel Principles: Trials, adversity, endurance

Scripture: D&C 121:7–9

Music: "Though Deepening Trials" (*Hymns*, no. 122), "Hum Your Favorite Hymn" (CS, 152)

Lesson:

President Kimball suffered many personal trials in his lifetime, so much so that he has been compared to the Old Testament prophet Job. Here is a sampling of the hardships he had to overcome:

During his childhood, President Kimball suffered from typhoid fever, smallpox, facial paralysis, and once nearly drowned.

When he was five, one of President Kimball's younger sisters died; his mother passed away when he was just eleven years old.

His life savings were wiped out in the Great Depression.

As a stake president, he had to care for many Saints whose homes were destroyed in floods.

In 1948, President Kimball suffered a heart attack. His heart condition resurfaced in 1972, requiring him to undergo open-heart surgery.

President Kimball battled recurring throat cancer, which led to one and a half of his vocal cords being removed. Afterward he was able to speak only with a hoarse whisper.

In *Faith Precedes the Miracle*, President Kimball wrote about trusting the Lord despite the trials and difficulties of this life:

"In the face of apparent tragedy we must put our trust in God, knowing that despite our limited view his purposes will not fail. With all its troubles life offers us the tremendous privilege to grow in knowledge and wisdom, faith and works, preparing to return and share God's glory."[100]

Activities:

1. Print a copy of "Activity Page 12.2: Adversity Puzzle" from the CD-ROM. After putting together the puzzle, discuss Elder Dieter F. Uchtdorf's quote and the blessings that can come into our lives from having challenges.

2. Write each of the following trials on separate slips of paper and place them into a container. Add other trials your family may have experienced. Take turns choosing a trial. Have the family member read what is written on the paper out loud and then comment on how he or she would respond faithfully to that specific challenge. Ask, "What do the responses have in common?"

Death of a loved one
Job loss
Loved one strays from the gospel
Natural disaster
Illness
A new, challenging calling
Strife with another
Divorce
Learning a new skill or language
Moving
Addiction
Separation from family

---

[100] Spencer W. Kimball, *Faith Precedes the Miracle* (Salt Lake City: Deseret Book, 1972), 105–106.

3. Provide each family member with a blank piece of paper and a writing utensil. Find a simple line drawing (or make one yourself) and have one family member give verbal instructions to the rest of the family as they try to draw it. The person giving the instructions or describing the picture is NOT allowed to show the original illustration to those who are drawing. After all family members are done drawing, have them show their pictures. Discuss the difficulties they had. Then compare this exercise to going through life. Remind family members that the Lord's view is not as limited as ours and that He will reach out to help us in times of need.

Additional Resources:

1. After the death of President Kimball, Ezra Taft Benson spoke in memory of Spencer W. Kimball's life, including trials he faced. The speech was published in the December 1985 *Ensign*.[101]

2. The gospel study section of www.lds.org has information on the topic of *adversity*, including scripture references, magazine articles, and other study materials.

3. A comic-book style rendition of Spencer W. Kimball's life challenges was published in the *Friend* magazine in October 2007.

---

[101] Ezra Taft Benson, "Spencer W. Kimball: A Star of the First Magnitude," *Ensign*, December 1985, 33.

Lesson 3: The Miracle of Forgiveness

Purpose: To help family members understand the importance of forgiveness, both forgiving others and seeking forgiveness from the Lord

Gospel Principles: Forgiveness, repentance, humility

Scripture: Matt. 11:28–30

Music: "In Humility" (*Hymns*, no. 172), "Help Me, Dear Father" (CS, 99)

Lesson:

When Spencer W. Kimball was first called to be a member of the Quorum of the Twelve Apostles, he felt extremely unworthy. He worried about living up to this calling and was determined to make things right with anyone he might have offended in his past. He visited many people in the process of explaining his situation—business partners, neighbors, those with whom he had served in the Church, and family members. He asked for forgiveness and sought to reconcile any mistakes he might have made in his life.[102] After he had done so, President Kimball felt more worthy to serve as an apostle.

The importance of repenting and seeking forgiveness continued to be a significant issue to President Kimball as a Church leader. During his service as an apostle he wrote the book *The Miracle of Forgiveness* (1969), which remains one of the bestselling books by a general authority today. *The Miracle of Forgiveness* outlines the following steps for repenting and achieving forgiveness:

---

[102] Edward L. Kimball and Andrew E. Kimball Jr., *Spencer W. Kimball: Twelfth President of The Church of Jesus Christ of Latter-day Saints* (Salt Lake City: Bookcraft Publishers, 1977), 197–198.

—Have sorrow for having committed sin
—Abandon the sin
—Confess the sin to God, to those personally affected by the sin, and to one's bishop (if necessary)
—Make restitution to the fullest extent possible
—Strive to keep the commandments

In addition to these steps, Elder Richard G. Scott adds, "Of all the necessary steps to repentance, I testify that the most critically important is for you to have a conviction that forgiveness comes because of the Redeemer. It is essential to know that only on His terms can you be forgiven."[103]

Activities:

1. Print a copy of "Activity Page 12.3: Who Am I?" from the CD-ROM. Ask family members if they can think of others in the scriptures who either forgave or were forgiven.

2. Pour a small amount of salt on a plate to represent an individual's purity. Sprinkle some pepper over the top to represents mistakes made. While explaining the symbolism of the salt and pepper and the necessity of the Atonement to achieve forgiveness, vigorously rub a plastic spoon on a part of clothing to generate static electricity. Explain that the Atonement helps to remove the impurities from our lives. Place the spoon over the salt and pepper; the pepper should be pulled up to the spoon by the static, making the salt pure again.[104] Testify that the Atonement has the ability to cleanse us if we are willing to repent.

---

[103] Richard G. Scott, "Finding Forgiveness," New Era, March 2010, 2–7.
[104] From www.kidssundayschool.com ("Harm Removed" by: Craig)

3. Using the *Teachings of Presidents of the Church: Spencer W. Kimball* (2006) manual, select a quote from *The Miracle of Forgiveness* (as included in Chapter 4) for each family member to read out loud and discuss.

Additional Resources:

1. The *Primary 2: CTRA* manual has a lesson on forgiving others; the lesson includes a coloring page as well as other suggested activities for younger children (see Lesson 40; available on www.lds.org).

2. Chapter 19 of the *Gospel Principles* manual (2009) is all about repentance and achieving forgiveness.

3. The 4:34-minute YouTube video *The Miracle of Forgiveness* (posted on quasar515 channel) was an entry for the International Video Contest sponsored by The Church of Jesus Christ of Latter-day Saints. It depicts a man's journey of repentance through Jesus Christ and the ultimate forgiveness he receives.

Ezra Taft Benson

CHAPTER THIRTEEN
EZRA TAFT BENSON

Introduction (Moroni 10:3-5)

Ezra Taft Benson served as the thirteenth president of the Church from 1985 to 1994. His service in the Church included serving as a stake president twice prior to being called as an apostle in 1943. Soon after this calling he was sent to Europe to distribute humanitarian aid and oversee the Church during the post-WWII transition period. President Benson is the only apostle to serve concurrently in the Church and in high public office (as Secretary of Agriculture under U. S. President Dwight D. Eisenhower). His close ties to agriculture stemmed from being raised on a farm in Idaho, receiving a master's degree in the field, and later working in the industry. As a prominent public and political figure, President Benson—along with his family—was often the subject of media scrutiny. Well-known for his love of the Book of Mormon and for his deep patriotism, President Benson regularly encouraged loyalty to God, family, and country. During the last few years of his life he was rarely seen in public due to failing health, entrusting daily operations of the Church to his counselors, Gordon B. Hinckley and Thomas S. Monson. He passed away in May 1994 and was buried near his birthplace in Whitney, Idaho.[105]

---

[105] Mark E. Petersen, "President Ezra Taft Benson," *Ensign*, January 1986, 2.

Ezra Taft Benson's Testimony of Jesus Christ

"I testify that Jesus is the Christ and that He stands at the head of His Church, even The Church of Jesus Christ of Latter-day Saints. I testify that he will come again in power and great glory and that He will leave nothing undone for our eternal welfare."[106]

Important Dates and Events in the Life of Ezra Taft Benson

Birth—August 4, 1899, in Whitney, Idaho

Parents—Sarah Dunkley and George T. Benson

Baptism—August 4, 1907 (age 8)

Mission—Great Britain (1921–1923)

Marriage—September 10, 1926, to Flora Smith Amussen

Children—6

Called as an Apostle—October 7, 1943 (age 44)

Ordained Prophet—November 10, 1985 (age 86)

Years as Prophet—8 years, 6 months

Death—May 30, 1994, in Salt Lake City, Utah

---

[106] As quoted in Richard Neitzel Holzapfel and William W. Slaughter, *Prophets of the Latter Days* (Salt Lake City: Deseret Book, 2003), 3.

Lesson 1: Beware of Pride

Purpose: To help family members understand the sin of pride and the importance of striving to be humble

Gospel Principles: Pride, enmity, humility

Scripture: Mormon 8:34–37

Music: "Be Thou Humble" (Hymns, no. 252), "Lord, I Would Follow Thee" (Hymns, no. 220)

Lesson:

"Pride is the universal sin, the great vice . . . the great stumbling block of Zion," taught President Ezra Taft Benson in one of his most famous conference talks.[107] President Benson felt the sin of pride was misunderstood and taught "there is no such thing as righteous pride. . . . Most of us think of pride as self-centeredness, conceit, boastfulness, arrogance, or haughtiness. All of these are elements of the sin, but the heart, or core, is still missing.

"The central feature of pride is enmity—enmity toward God and enmity toward our fellowmen. *Enmity* means 'hatred toward, hostility to, or a state of opposition.'" He also taught that disobedience, contention, and taking offense are all characteristic of those with pride.

President Benson explained the way to overcome pride is by learning to be humble. He stated, "The antidote for pride is humility—meekness, submissiveness. It is the broken heart and contrite spirit." He then went on to provide eight different ways we can be humble:

---

[107] Ezra Taft Benson, "Beware of Pride," *Ensign*, May 1989, 4.

"We can choose to humble ourselves by conquering enmity toward [others].

"We can choose to humble ourselves by receiving counsel and chastisement.

"We can choose to humble ourselves by forgiving those who have offended us.

"We can choose to humble ourselves by rendering selfless service.

"We can choose to humble ourselves by [doing missionary work].

"We can choose to humble ourselves by getting to the temple more frequently.

"We can choose to humble ourselves by confessing and forsaking our sins.

"We can choose to humble ourselves by loving God, submitting our will to His, and putting Him first in our lives."

Activities:

1. Print a copy of "Activity Page 13.1: Ottendorf Pride Cipher" from the CD-ROM. Work together to find the hidden message taken from President Benson's address on pride.

2. Before reading the lesson above, play a game of limbo. Use a broom or mop handle for the bar and gradually move it lower to see who can bend the lowest to get under without falling over. After playing the game, discuss pride and its remedy, humility. Tell family members sometimes being humble can be difficult. Ask how the game of limbo is like being prideful or humble.

3. Teach family members the story of the Tower of Babel (see Gen. 10 and 11:1–9), including the brother of Jared's prayerfulness and humility (see Ether 1:33–37). Emphasize that most of the people were so prideful of their own capabilities they thought they could build their tower tall enough to reach heaven. It was only humility that allowed Jared's people to be able to communicate with each other. Use blocks or Legos® to build towers; see who can build the tallest tower before it collapses.

Additional Resources:

1. Love God, love your brothers and sisters, give selfless service, forgive, confess and repent of our sins, and be open to counsel are some practical applications the *New Era* published to help individuals be more humble.[108]

2. The Book of Mormon seminary teacher resource manual has a picture of the Tower of Babel story; it is available online at www.seminary.lds.org.

3. A helpful coloring and quiz sheet about the Tower of Babel story was published in the January 1990 *Friend* magazine.

---

[108] "Idea List: Fighting Pride," *New Era*, February 2002, 15.

Lesson 2: The Book of Mormon

Purpose: To help family members understand the significant role the Book of Mormon plays as the "keystone of our religion"

Gospel Principles: Book of Mormon, scripture, testimony

Scripture: D&C 84:54–58

Music: "An Angel from on High" (*Hymns*, no. 13), "Book of Mormon Stories" (CS, 118)

Lesson:

In the summer of 1921, at the age of twenty-two, Ezra Taft Benson was called on a mission to Great Britain. Despite his willingness to work and serve diligently, he found missionary work to be challenging. Young Elder Benson recorded in his journal that he was frustrated with his poor public speaking skills, what he called his "frail attempt at speaking."

At one point, though, Elder Benson was invited to give a talk about apostasy but instead felt inspired to speak on the Book of Mormon. He later described this experience, saying, "I spoke with a freedom I had never experienced. Afterward, I couldn't recall what I had said, but several nonmembers surrounded me and said, 'Tonight we received a witness that Joseph Smith was a prophet of God, and we are ready for baptism.' . . . I knew that the Lord was with me."[109]

From this point on, Ezra Taft Benson had a testimony of the importance of the Book of Mormon to the gospel. After becoming prophet, President Benson testified greatly of the Book of Mormon, calling it the "keystone of our religion" and

---

[109] Sheri L. Dew, *Ezra Taft Benson: A Biography* (Salt Lake City: Deseret Book, 1987), 55.

urging members to "flood the earth" with it.[110] Since then, thousands have increased their testimonies of the gospel because they are studying and following the teachings of the Book of Mormon as President Benson requested.[111] And the earth is being flooded with the Book of Mormon—more than 150 million copies have now been printed in more than 100 languages. Additionally, the Book of Mormon is available online for access to millions worldwide.

Activities:

1. Print a copy of "Activity Page 13.2: Keystone of Our Religion" from the CD-ROM. Use this activity page to demonstrate how a keystone in an arch works as well as to discuss the importance of the Book of Mormon in having a testimony of the gospel.

2. Watch the "Family Home Evening Video Supplement— 'Flood the Earth with the Book of Mormon,'" 5:50 minutes (Video Clip 2, available through the online www.LDS.org store), or "The Book of Mormon: A Book with a Promise," one of the Mormon Messages posted on YouTube (as posted on the MormonMessages channel). After viewing, take time to have family members write their personal testimony in copies of the Book of Mormon. Share these books with a nonmember directly or give them to a missionary to share.

Additional Resources:

1. The visitors' centers of the Church often have a display of the Book of Mormon in many of the different languages in which it has been printed. Try to visit a display; while there

---

[110] Ezra Taft Benson, "The Keystone of Our Religion," *Ensign*, January 1992, 2.
[111] J. Ballard Washburn, "Follow the Prophet," *Friend*, October 1991, inside front cover.

you may want to take the opportunity to watch the classic LDS film, "How Rare a Possession," which testifies of the power of the Book of Mormon.

2. The blog indybooks.blogspot.com ("Flooding the Earth with the Book of Mormon") has regular posts about experiences individuals have sharing the Book of Mormon. These stories may provide ideas on how your family can share the Book of Mormon.

3. Sugardoodle.net has numerous Book of Mormon resources (such as clipart, reading charts, games, jokes, and videos) that might be helpful.

Lesson 3: Love of Country

Purpose: To teach family members how they can help improve their community and nation

Gospel Principles: Patriotism, citizenship, government

Scripture: D&C 134:1

Music: "The Star-Spangled Banner" (*Hymns*, no. 340, or your own national anthem), "My Country" (CS, 224)

Lesson:

President Ezra Taft Benson spent eight years as the Secretary of Agriculture in the administration of U. S. President Dwight D. Eisenhower. He was chosen for this position because of his love of free enterprise and his reputation for being a man of principle. President Benson was very patriotic and devoted to liberty. He even wrote his own political creed: "I am for freedom and against slavery. I am for social progress and against socialism. I am for a dynamic economy and against waste. I am for the private competitive market and against unnecessary governmental intervention. I am for national security and against appeasement and capitulation to an obvious enemy."[112]

Later, while serving as an apostle, Elder Benson gave advice on improving communities and nations. He wrote, "Now you ask what you can do as one individual or family to influence your community . . .? I know of no better question a citizen could ask himself than that. May I suggest a few things which I believe would be beneficial."

---

[112] Kenneth W. Godfrey, "Ezra Taft Benson," *Utah History Encyclopedia* (Salt Lake City: University of Utah Press, 1994), 40–41.

1. Keep your own families strong. A nation is no stronger than the sum total of its families.

2. Live by the fundamental principles of work, thrift, and self-reliance and teach children by example.

3. Learn about the Constitution, the Declaration of Independence, and other basic government documents; the greatest watchdog of freedom is an informed electorate.

4. Seek out good, wise, and honest men for public office, and then support them with your vote.

5. Heed strictly the commandments of God, particularly the *Ten Commandments*. As long as we regard God as our Sovereign and uphold His laws, we shall be free from bondage and be protected.[113]

Activities:

1. Print a copy of "Activity Page 13.3: Stars of Citizenship" from the CD-ROM. Use the activity page to reinforce the five principles of being a good citizen as taught by President Benson.

2. Have family members draw, color, or make a collage of your state or national flag. Display the flags in a front window. Discuss how the flag is a symbol of patriotism. Ask family members to name other ways they can show or increase their patriotism.

3. Go on a field trip to visit an important historical site in your community. If possible, take a tour or learn about its significance and relevance to current times.

---

[113] Ezra Taft Benson, "America at the Crossroads," *New Era*, July 1978, 36.

Additional Resources:

1. Robert K. and Shirley Wilkes Thomas wrote the helpful article "Declaration of Dependence: Teaching Patriotism in the Home," which was published in the June 1976 *Ensign*. As this was the bicentennial year for the United States, numerous articles related to patriotism were published in Church magazines.

2. A "Patriotism Quiz" was published in the July 1974 *Friend*. Similarly, "Patriots Speak!" is another quiz published in the February 1976 *Friend*.

3. A number of patriotic messages have been given as part of the Mormon Tabernacle Choir's "Music and the Spoken Word" series. For transcripts of these messages, search "patriotism" on the website www.musicandthespokenword. com/messages.

Howard W. Hunter

CHAPTER FOURTEEN
HOWARD W. HUNTER

Introduction (John 13:34)

Howard W. Hunter was the fourteenth president of the Church, serving from 1994 to 1995. He was the first latter-day prophet born in the twentieth century, and his nine-month duration of leadership is the briefest in the history of the Church. Born and raised in Idaho to Scottish immigrant parents, Howard W. Hunter was from a part-member family. His mother diligently raised him in the gospel; it wasn't until Howard was an adult that his father joined the Church. President Hunter worked at a number of jobs (including professional musician, bridge painter, banker, title examiner, and laundry detergent salesman) before going to law school in California. After serving as a bishop and stake president he was called to be an apostle in 1959. Elder Hunter participated in a number of significant activities during his apostolic years, including developing the Polynesian Cultural Center in Hawaii and acquiring land to build the BYU Jerusalem Center. At age eighty-six he became prophet and encouraged the Latter-day Saints to be temple-worthy and live Christ-like lives.

Howard W. Hunter's Testimony of Jesus Christ

"I bear solemn and grateful witness that Jesus is the Christ, the Savior of the world. Certainly He is the center of our worship and the key to our happiness. Let us follow the Son of God in all ways and all walks of life. Let us make Him our exemplar and our guide."[114]

Important Dates and Events in the Life of Howard W. Hunter

Birth—November 14, 1907, in Boise, Idaho

Parents—Nellie Marie Rasmussen and John William Hunter

Baptism—April 4, 1920 (age 12)

Mission—None

Marriage—June 10, 1931, to Clara May Jeffs (first wife)

Children—2

Called as an Apostle—October 15, 1959 (age 51)

Ordained Prophet—June 5, 1994 (age 86)

Years as Prophet—9 months

Death—March 3, 1995, in Salt Lake City, Utah

---

[114] Howard W. Hunter, "Follow the Son of God," Ensign, November 1994, 87.

Lesson 1: Love of Music

Purpose: To help family members appreciate music and the enrichment musical talents can bring to life

Gospel Principles: Music, singing, developing talents

Scripture: D&C 136:28

Music: "Come Sing to the Lord" (*Hymns*, no. 10), "Sing Your Way Home" (CS, 193)

Lesson:

Howard W. Hunter loved music, played at least seven instruments, and even started his own orchestra, which he named "Hunter's Croonaders." His sister Dorothy recalled, "My mother said that from the time he was a baby, 'he always kept perfect time' to music . . . 'He has perfect pitch,' she [said], and 'a beautiful voice.'"[115]

Hunter's Croonaders became a popular group, playing more than fifty engagements in 1925. Then, in 1926, Howard had the opportunity to form a five-member orchestra to play on the *SS President Jackson*, a cruise ship headed to the Orient for two months. The group played popular music during the lunch hour, classical music during dinner, dance music in the ballroom, and background music to accompany silent movies.[116]

President Hunter gave up playing music professionally when he got married. He did not feel the life of a musician was conducive to family life, especially considering the poor economy during the Depression. Despite this, he sustained his love of music and shared his musical talents with family for the rest of his life.

---

[115] *The Presidents of the Church: Howard W. Hunter*, 235.
[116] *Ibid.*, 236.

Activities:

1. Print a copy of "Activity Page 14.1: Musical Instrument Puzzler" from the CD-ROM. Use this worksheet as a starting point to learn about different musical instruments. Look up various types of instruments in an encyclopedia or on the Internet to learn more about how they are played and what type of sound they make.

2. Ask family members ahead of time to prepare a talent to share, especially a musical talent, if possible. If family members are not musically inclined, take time during family home evening to sing songs or demonstrate an instrument. You could also use the introduction of *Hymns* to teach family members how to lead music.

Additional Resources:

1. A photograph of Howard W. Hunter's orchestra, Hunter's Croonaders, is available online at www.institute.lds.org.

2. A *Friend* cartoon illustration of President Hunter's many jobs includes his time as a professional musician (November 2001).

3. The Church music website (www.lds.org/churchmusic) is helpful in learning new music. There is an interactive music player, options for downloading music, and additional educational materials available for use.

Lesson 2: Temple Worthiness

Purpose: To help family members understand the importance of being worthy to hold a temple recommend

Gospel Principles: Temple recommends, personal worthiness, integrity

Scripture: D&C 72:19

Music: "More Holiness Give Me" (*Hymns*, no. 131), "I Will Follow God's Plan" (CS, 164)

Lesson:

Each temple is a very special and holy place, sometimes called the "House of the Lord." One of the ways temples are kept holy is through the use of temple recommends. To show worthiness, Church members must first be interviewed by a member of their bishopric (or branch presidency) and stake presidency; if found worthy, they receive a signed paper called a temple recommend. Recommends must be renewed every two years. Every time members go to the temple they must show their temple recommend at the front desk. Only worthy temple recommend holders are allowed inside because they have been found clean and have promised to treat the temple and its ordinances sacredly.

As the newly set-apart prophet, President Howard W. Hunter made clear one of his goals for the Latter-day Saints: increasing temple worthiness. He invited the "members of the Church to establish the temple of the Lord as the great symbol of their membership and the supernal setting for their most sacred covenants." He also emphasized, "It would be the deepest desire of my heart to have every member of the Church be temple worthy. I would hope that every adult member would be worthy of—and carry—a current temple recommend, even if proximity to a temple does not allow immediate or frequent use of it."[117]

Activities:

1. Print a copy of "Activity Page 14.2: Temple-Attending People Viewer" from the CD-ROM. Have family members color the pictures and put together the view slider as you discuss the various rooms in the temple

2. Review with family members some of the questions asked during a temple recommend interview (shown below). Have a family member role-play a member of the bishopric interviewing someone for a temple recommend.

—Do you have faith in and a testimony of God the Eternal Father, His Son Jesus Christ, and the Holy Ghost?

—Do you have a testimony of the Atonement of Christ and of His role as Savior and Redeemer?

—Do you have a testimony of the restoration of the gospel in these the latter days?

—Are you a full-tithe payer?

—Are you honest in all your dealings with your fellowmen?

—Do you keep the Word of Wisdom?

Additional Resources:

1. Boyd K. Packer, author of *The Holy Temple* (Salt Lake City: Bookcraft, 1980), wrote an *Ensign* article describing the importance of temple worthiness and recommends (February 1995 issue).

---

[117] *The Presidents of the Church: Howard W. Hunter*, 251.

2. "Your Temple Recommend" is a *New Era* article written by President Howard W. Hunter. In it he reviewed what qualifies someone for a temple recommend (April 1995 issue).

3. Sugardoodle.net has a pattern for a temple recommend holder family members could make as a craft. There is also a printable handout of a "recommend" for future temple patrons (ideal for children).

Lesson 3: The Christ-Centered Life

Purpose: To teach family members the importance of focusing our lives on the example and teachings of Jesus Christ

Gospel Principles: Jesus Christ—example, faith, commitment

Scripture: 2 Ne. 25:26

Music: "I Believe in Christ" (*Hymns*, no. 134), "Tell Me the Stories of Jesus" (CS, 57)

Lesson:

President Howard W. Hunter loved the Savior and often taught the Saints to follow the Lord's teachings and example in their lives. As a stake president, he was concerned about all of those in his care and encouraged the stake and ward leaders to seek out those who needed particular reassurance and support. President Hunter also started a class to help struggling members. The class emphasized improving personal relationships with God and Jesus Christ. Many of the students who attended the class became active members of the Church and went to the temple.[118]

While serving as the president of the Quorum of the Twelve, President Hunter taught Brigham Young University students to focus their lives on the Savior, stating, "Please remember this one thing. If our lives and our faith are centered upon Jesus Christ and his restored gospel, nothing can ever go permanently wrong. On the other hand, if our lives are not

---

[118] Eleanor Knowles, *Howard W. Hunter* (Salt Lake City: Deseret Book Company, 1994), 136.

centered on the Savior and his teachings, no other success can ever be permanently right."[119]

After being sustained as prophet, President Hunter invited "all members of the Church to live with ever more attention to the life and example of the Lord Jesus Christ, especially the love and hope and compassion He displayed."

Activities:

1. Print a copy of "Activity Page 14.3: Christ-Centered Maze" from the CD-ROM. Ask family members how they can make Christ the center of their life, even when they feel lost or alone.

2. Go to www.JesusChrist.lds.org to watch the video *Finding Faith in Christ* (under the multimedia section; this video is also available in most meetinghouse libraries). Discuss how being focused on the Savior can help us live more peaceful, fulfilling lives in the last days.

3. Review the following four specific steps for being Christ-like in our relationships with others. Have family members write and perform a mini skit that exemplifies using these steps.

—Seek the spirit of Christ through scripture study, prayer, and service.

—Remember that everyone is a child of God; treat each one accordingly.

—Live the "Golden Rule" by being kind and considerate of others.

---

[119] "Fear Not, Little Flock," *Brigham Young University 1988–89 Devotional and Fireside Speeches* (1989), 112.

—Be willing to change and apologize if you make a mistake.[120]

Additional Resources:

1. Read the *Ensign* article "The Christ-Centered Life," written by Neal A. Maxwell (August 1981), to learn twelve tactics to utilize in focusing more on the Savior.

2. If giving this lesson at Easter or Christmas, suggestions for making the holiday more Christ-centered can be found on Sugardoodle.net.

3. The Gospel Art Kit has numerous pictures of the Savior that can be used for this lesson or to display in the home. The pictures can be printed for free online (search Gospel Art Kit on www.lds.org).

---

[120] "How to Be More Christ-centered in Our Relationships with Others," *Church News*, December 21, 1996, back cover.

Gordon B. Hinckley

CHAPTER FIFTEEN
GORDON B. HINCKLEY

Introduction (D&C 110:7)

The fifteenth president of The Church of Jesus Christ of Latter-day Saints was Gordon Bitner Hinckley. As a fourth-generation member of the Church, President Hinckley was raised in Salt Lake City by faithful parents. He attended college and served a mission in Great Britain. Afterward, he used his journalism degree to gain employment as executive secretary of the Radio, Publicity, and Missionary Literature Committee of the Church. President Hinckley served as a stake president and as assistant to the Quorum of the Twelve before being called as an apostle in 1961. He served in the First Presidency from 1981 until he was sustained as prophet in 1995, an experience that was particularly beneficial in preparing him to lead the Church. During Gordon B. Hinckley's administration he built the Conference Center, doubled the number of temples, raised the bar for missionary work, expanded the media (including Internet) outreach of the Church, started the Perpetual Education Fund, and released *The Family: A Proclamation to the World*. Additionally, Church membership grew from 9.3 million to more than 13 million under his leadership.[121]

---

[121] "LDS President Gordon B. Hinckley Dies at Age 97," *Deseret News*, January 28, 2008.

Gordon B. Hinckley's Testimony of Jesus Christ

"Jesus is the Christ, His immortal Son, who under His Father's direction was the Creator of the earth. He was the great Jehovah of the Old Testament, who condescended to come into the world as the Messiah, who gave His life on Calvary's cross in His wondrous Atonement because He loved us. The work in which we are engaged is their work, and we are their servants, who are answerable to them."[122]

Important Dates and Events in the Life of Gordon B. Hinckley

Birth—June 23, 1910, in Salt Lake City, Utah

Parents—Ada Bitner and Bryant Stringham Hinckley

Baptism—April 28, 1919 (age 8)

Mission—British Isles (1933–1935)

Marriage—April 29, 1937, to Marjorie Pay

Children—5

Called as an Apostle—October 5, 1961 (age 51)

Ordained Prophet—March 12, 1995 (age 84)

Years as Prophet—12 years, 10 months

Death—January 27, 2008, in Salt Lake City, Utah

---

[122] Gordon B. Hinckley, "Testimony," *Ensign*, May 1998, 71.

Lesson 1: The Six "Be"s

Purpose: To help family members understand some of the basic characteristics they can develop to improve their character and make their lives more rewarding

Gospel Principles: Gratitude, humility, integrity

Scripture: D&C 59:9

Music: "True to the Faith" (*Hymns*, no. 254), "I Need My Heavenly Father" (CS, 18)

Lesson:

In November 2000, President Hinckley gave an address to young single adults from the Conference Center. His remarks, also broadcast throughout the Church, gave youth some inspirational, down-to-earth advice to help them be more "fruitful" in their lives. His memorable advice became known as "The Six 'Be's":

Be grateful. Express appreciation to everyone who does us a favor or assists us in any way (see D&C 59:21).

Be smart. The Lord wants us to train our minds and hands to become an influence for good (see D&C 88:78–80).

Be clean. We live in a world filled with filth and sleaze. We cannot afford to let it touch us. We should not be disrespectful of the body the Lord has given us (see 1 Cor. 3:16-17).

Be true. Let us be loyal to the Church under all circumstances. The authorities of this Church will lead us in paths of happiness (see 1 Tim. 4:12).

Be humble. The meek and the humble are those who are teachable (see Matt. 5:5).

Be prayerful. Look to the Lord for understanding and guidance, and walk according to His precepts and commandments (see D&C 10:5).[123]

Note: President Hinckley later added three more "Be"s in his book *Way to Be*—be involved, be still, and be positive.

Activities:

1. Print a copy of "Activity Page 15.1: The Six 'Be's Door Hangers" from the CD-ROM. Hang on a door as a reminder of President Hinckley's counsel.

2. Using Gospel Art Pictures 221 (be grateful), 617 (be smart), 110 (be clean), 117 (be true), 105 (be humble), and 605 (be prayerful), play a game of matching. Show family members one of the pictures at a time and see if they can determine which of the "Six 'Be's" it best represents.

Additional Resources:

1. www.lds.about.com has a "Six 'Be's" .pdf file that can be folded into a booklet as a handout. There are also bookmarks and a chart that can be printed.

2. Janice Kapp Perry has written music to teach the "Six B"s. The music is found on the album *When a Prophet Speaks.*

3. A "Six Be"s free, printable flashcard flipbook is available on ayearoffhe.blogspot.com (as part of an April 2011 lesson).

---

[123] Gordon B. Hinckley, "A Prophet's Counsel and Prayer for Youth," *Ensign,* January 2001, 2.

Lesson 2: The Family: A Proclamation to the World

Purpose: To help family members learn how the family can be strengthened by utilizing the teachings found in *The Family: A Proclamation to the World*

Gospel Principles: Family, divine nature, marriage

Scripture: Mosiah 2:41

Music: "For the Beauty of the Earth" (*Hymns*, no. 92), "The Family is of God" (published in the October 2008 *Friend*)

Lesson:

During the annual General Relief Society meeting on September 23, 1995, President Gordon B. Hinckley first presented *The Family: A Proclamation to the World*, a statement by the First Presidency and Quorum of the Twelve reaffirming the sanctity of the family and marriage. Addressed to all nations, the proclamation has become an important document for guiding and strengthening families in a challenging world.

In introducing the proclamation, President Hinckley stated, "With so much of sophistry that is passed off as truth, with so much of deception concerning standards and values, with so much of allurement and enticement to take on the slow stain of the world, we have felt to warn and forewarn." He also stated, "We commend to all a careful, thoughtful, and prayerful reading of this proclamation. The strength of any nation is rooted within the walls of its homes. We urge our people everywhere to strengthen their families in conformity with these time-honored values."[124]

---

[124] Gordon B. Hinckley, "Stand Strong against the Wiles of the World," *Ensign*, November 1995, 98.

Since its presentation, *The Family: A Proclamation to the World* has been translated into seventy-seven languages and presented to the leaders of nations around the world.

Activities:

1. Print a copy of "Activity Page 15.2: Our Family" from the CD-ROM. Use this coloring page to have family members draw or write a description of each of the principles listed in the seventh paragraph of the proclamation. Select one or two of these principles and set a goal as a family to do something in the upcoming week in that area. Give an assignment to each family member as part of the goal.

2. Obtain a copy of *The Family: A Proclamation to the World* to hang in your home (available online for free). Find a mat and frame in which to place it. Decorate the mat by making a collage with family photos or other craft items.

Additional Resources:

1. *Doctrine and Covenants and Church History Video Presentations* (53912), a DVD prepared for use in teaching Sunday School, has a seven-minute segment entitled "Responsibility of Parents."

2. A .pdf crossword puzzle based on the wording of *The Family: A Proclamation to the World* is available for use on www.lds.about.com.

3. Visit www.familyproclamationweek.com for a number of helpful resources, ideas, and activities. This site invites families to sign up to participate in a special week where they focus on each other and give undivided attention to family members for seven days.

Lesson 3: Builder of Temples

Purpose: To teach family members the importance of temples

Gospel Principles: Temples, house of the Lord, revelation

Scripture: 1 Kgs. 9:3

Music: "High on the Mountain Top" (*Hymns*, no. 5), "Beauty Everywhere" (CS, 232)

Lesson:

For the first 150 years of the Church, temple construction was slow and purposeful. Temples were usually built only when membership in an area was able to support or sustain the number of volunteers needed to run the temple as well as provide a sufficient number of patrons. But in 1997, President Gordon B. Hinckley had the desire to extend temple blessings to more Church members, particularly in remote parts of the world. After pondering and praying about this desire, he received the revelation to build smaller temples that would require fewer resources and funds. With only fifty operating temples and two years before the turn of the century, President Hinckley then set an ambitious goal to double the number of temples by the year 2000. This goal was achieved when on October 1, 2000, the one hundredth temple was dedicated in Boston, Massachusetts.

After reaching this goal, President Hinckley continued to have temples built, one of the most important being the rebuilding of the Nauvoo Illinois Temple. At the time of his death there were 138 temples in operation, under construction, or in planning stages. The lives of Latter-day Saints around the world were blessed by Gordon B. Hinckley's vision and leadership.

Activities:

1. Print a copy of "Activity Page 15.3: Temple Expertise" from the CD-ROM.

2. After reading the above lesson, have family members make a collage of modern-day temple pictures by cutting photographs out of Church magazines or printing pictures from the Internet.

3. Play "Temples Dot the Earth," a card game published in the November 2002 *Friend* magazine.

Additional Resources:

1. Visit www.lds.org/church/temples to learn about current operating temples, to see what temples are under construction, to determine whether any new temples have been announced, and to discover if any open houses or dedications are planned nearby.

2. Heather Kirby and Paul E. Koelliker wrote "Blessings of the Temple," a story about temples being built (July 2007 *Friend*).

Thomas S. Monson

CHAPTER SIXTEEN
THOMAS S. MONSON

Introduction (1 Chron. 29:5)

Thomas S. Monson was born in Salt Lake City, Utah, in 1927, the second of six children in Spencer and Gladys Monson's tight-knit family. At age seventeen he served in the United States Navy near the close of World War II but was never sent into action. A printer by trade, President Monson has devoted most of his life to church and community service. In 1950, at age twenty-two, he was called as a bishop in Salt Lake City. At age twenty-seven, he became a counselor in a stake presidency, and at age thirty-one he became a mission president in Canada. By age thirty-six, Thomas S. Monson was sustained as the newest member of the Quorum of the Twelve Apostles. He served as a counselor in the First Presidency beginning in 1985, assisting Presidents Ezra Taft Benson, Howard W. Hunter, and Gordon B. Hinckley.[125] Well known for his storytelling speaking style, President Monson was sustained as prophet in 2008. Since then he has continued the pace of temple building and distribution of humanitarian aid around the world, dedicated the new Church Historical Library and Archives, and has affirmed a strong stance in support of traditional marriage and the family.

---

[125] "President Thomas S. Monson," retrieved July 3, 2011, from http://newsroom.lds.org/leader-biographies/president-thomas-s-monson

Thomas S. Monson's Testimony of Jesus Christ

"With all my heart and the fervency of my soul, I lift up my voice in testimony as a special witness and declare that God does live. Jesus is His Son, the Only Begotten of the Father in the flesh. He is our Redeemer; He is our Mediator with the Father. He it was who died on the cross to atone for our sins. He became the firstfruits of the Resurrection. Because He died, all shall live again. 'Oh, sweet the joy this sentence gives: "I know that my Redeemer lives!"' May the whole world know it and live by that knowledge."[126]

Important Dates and Events in the Life of Thomas S. Monson

Birth—August 21, 1927, in Salt Lake City, Utah

Parents—Gladys Condie and G. Spencer Monson

Baptism—September 28, 1935 (age 8)

Mission—President of Canadian Mission (1959–1962)

Marriage—October 7, 1948, to Frances Beverly Johnson

Children—3

Called as an Apostle—October 10, 1963 (age 36)

Ordained Prophet—February 3, 2008 (age 80)

Years as Prophet—Current

---

[126] Thomas S. Monson, "I Know That My Redeemer Lives!," *Ensign*, May 2007, 25.

Lesson 1: Developing Talents

Purpose: To encourage family members to develop personal interests and talents

Gospel Principles: Talents, self-improvement, work

Scripture: D&C 82:18

Music: "Improve the Shining Moments" (*Hymns*, no. 226), "Every Star Is Different" (CS, 142)

Lesson:

President Monson has worked diligently to develop many different talents. One of his talents is being a pigeon keeper. At about age eleven, young Tommy Monson began what would become a lifelong fascination with pigeons. Using a simple box trap, he and his friends caught some common pigeons (called "commies") in the backyard. Later, neighbor John Fife gave Tommy his first pair of Birmingham rollers, a popular breed of domesticated pigeons that can do rapid backward somersaults while in flight. Tommy worked hard to build a coop for his pigeons from scrap wood. And he bought more pigeons by earning money from sweeping up leftover kernels of wheat lodged in the nooks and crannies of boxcars. Tommy did all this despite the fact his father considered the hobby to be too expensive and a waste of time. Eventually Tom began showing his pigeons at county and state fairs, winning ribbons as he became more proficient at breeding and raising Birmingham rollers. In 1964, in his late thirties, his rollers swept the county fair, winning the trophy for the most superior young pigeon and a rosette for the most outstanding old bird.[127] Throughout

---

[127] Heidi S. Swinton, *To the Rescue: The Biography of Thomas S. Monson* (Salt Lake City: Deseret Book, 2010), 41–43.

his life President Monson has continued his hobby of pigeon keeping and still enjoys visiting the county and state fairs to meet with other pigeon fanciers. No matter what the talent, President Monson has taught, "Don't forget: one of the saddest things in life is wasted talent."[128]

Activities:

1. Print a copy of "Activity Page 16.1: Homing Pigeon Maze" from the CD-ROM.

2. Have each family member prepare a talent he or she can share with the rest of the family during family home evening. Take the opportunity to praise and encourage each other for efforts made to develop these talents.

Additional Resources:

1. Chapter 34 of the Gospel Principles manual is all about developing talents; similar lessons are found in the Young Women and priesthood manuals.

2. The Faith in God program for Primary children gives a number of suggested activities for children to help develop their talents. To earn the Faith in God award, children must accomplish two of these during the course of each year between ages eight and twelve.

3. The parable of the talents (see Matt. 25:14–30) is a great scripture story illustrating the importance of developing talents. A coloring page of this parable can be found on the website www.sermons4kids.com.

---

[128] Thomas S. Monson, "Three Gates Only You Can Open," New Era, August 2008, 2–6.

Lesson 2: Charity

Purpose: To help family members understand the importance of developing the quality of Christ-like charity

Gospel Principles: Charity, service, humility

Scripture: Mosiah 2:17

Music: "Love One Another" (*Hymns*, no. 308), "'Give,' Said the Little Stream" (CS, 236)

Lesson:

President Monson has taught throughout his life that loving and serving others with a Christ-like attitude is an essential part of living an honorable, even successful life. Further, he has encouraged Latter-day Saints to "Fill your life with service . . . that commodity of such priceless value."[129]

Of course, President Monson has given much service in his own personal life. At the young age of twenty-two, Thomas S. Monson was called to serve as the bishop of the Salt Lake City Sixty-Seventh Ward. Bishop Monson oversaw the care of more than a thousand ward members, including eighty-four widows. At Christmas time each year he would make a personal visit to each of the eighty-four widows, delivering a gift and giving each a blessing. This special act of service usually required Bishop Monson take a week of personal vacation from work to accomplish. But every year he did so, and continued to do so, even after he was released as bishop. Eventually, President Monson spoke at each of the funerals of these eighty-four widows, demonstrating loving care for each individual one.[130]

---

[129] Thomas S. Monson, "Formula for Success," *Ensign*, March 1996, 2.
[130] Francis M. Gibbons, "President Thomas S. Monson," *Ensign*, July 1995, 6.

Activities:

1. Print a copy of "Activity Page 16.2: Secret Service Message" from the CD-ROM.

2. Make a visit to a widow(er) in your neighborhood. Take a treat and spend time visiting and getting to know her/him. Other service ideas for assisting senior citizens may include visiting a nursing home, picking up the mail or newspaper and bringing it to the door, checking on senior citizens during bad weather conditions, delivering a meal to a homebound individual, or offering to read to or play a game with him/her.

Additional Resources:

1. The Mormon Messages channel on YouTube.com has posted a video entitled, "President Thomas S. Monson—Charity Never Faileth" (approximately twenty minutes long). Taken from his remarks at a Relief Society broadcast, the video features President Monson discussing charity, service, and visiting the widows and speaking at their funerals.

2. There are several scripture stories about widows that could be shared, including the widow of Zarephath (see 1 Kgs. 17) and the widow of Nain (see Luke 7:11–15). Both of these scripture stories are highlighted in an *Ensign* article written by President Monson in 2003.[131]

3. A May 2008 *Friend* article has a brief biographical sketch of President Monson that mentions his care of the eighty-four widows.

---

[131] Thomas S. Monson, "The Fatherless and the Widows: Beloved of God," *Ensign*, August 2003, 2–7.

Lesson 3: Cultivating Gratitude

Purpose: To help family members understand the importance of cultivating gratitude in their daily lives

Gospel Principles: Gratitude, thanksgiving, love

Scripture: Luke 17:11–19

Music: "Come Ye Thankful People" (*Hymns*, no. 94), "I Thank Thee, Dear Father" (CS, 7)

Lesson:

Early during his service as prophet, President Monson emphasized the importance of gratitude in a conference address, saying, "My brothers and sisters, do we remember to give thanks for the blessings we receive? Sincerely giving thanks not only helps us recognize our blessings, but it also unlocks the doors of heaven and helps us feel God's love . . .

"Gratitude is a divine principle. . . . Regardless of our circumstances, each of us has much for which to be grateful if we will but pause and contemplate our blessings. . . . We can lift ourselves and others as well when we refuse to remain in the realm of negative thought and cultivate within our hearts an attitude of gratitude. If ingratitude be numbered among the serious sins, then gratitude takes its place among the noblest of virtues. . . .

"How can we cultivate within our hearts an attitude of gratitude? . . . A grateful heart . . . comes through expressing gratitude to our Heavenly Father for His blessings and to those around us for all that they bring into our lives. This requires conscious effort—at least until we have truly learned and cultivated an attitude of gratitude. Often we feel grateful and *intend* to express our thanks but forget to do so or just don't get around to it. Someone has said that 'feeling gratitude and not expressing it is like wrapping a present and not giving it.'

"My brothers and sisters, to express gratitude is gracious and honorable, to enact gratitude is generous and noble, but to live with gratitude ever in our hearts is to touch heaven."[132]

Activities:

1. Print a copy of "Activity Page 16.3: Thank-You Cards Coloring Page" from the CD-ROM. Take time to express gratitude to others by writing on these thank-you notes or taking a treat to someone.

2. Read the story of the ten lepers as found in Luke (see Luke 17:11–19; use Gospel Art Kit 221 as a visual aid). President Monson taught that those who were healed from leprosy were given a new lease on life, and that He was disappointed in the nine who failed to demonstrate gratitude. Ask family members if are there instances in life where the Lord has blessed us, but we have failed to recognize and express our gratitude. Could the Lord be disappointed in us as well?

Additional Resources:

1. President Monson's conference talk (as referenced below) also contains a touching story about gratitude felt by members of the Green family despite their difficult financial situation.

2. Go online to www.hallmark.com to get tips on writing a sincere thank-you note (found under the **Thank You** tab and **Appreciation Ideas**).

---

[132] Thomas S. Monson, "The Divine Gift of Gratitude," *Ensign*, November 2010, 87–90.

Lesson 4: Follow the Prophet

Purpose: To teach family members the importance of following the living prophet to journey safely through our time on earth

Gospel Principles: Obedience, revelation, guidance

Scripture: 1 Kgs. 9:3

Music: "We Thank Thee, O God, for a Prophet" (*Hymns*, no. 19), "Follow the Prophet" (CS, 110)

Lesson:

President Thomas S. Monson became prophet in February 2008 after a lifetime of service and divine preparation. Just as getting on the ark was important to those who lived in the days of Noah, or being willing to leave their home behind was important when Lehi left Jerusalem, following the counsel of President Monson will help us live safer, happier lives.

In the May 2006 *Friend*, President Monson gave specific guidance to help lead us to safety, giving six suggestions that he called "a road map to safety." Access the article at "Come Listen to a Prophet's Voice: Follow the Signs" on pages 2–3 and share the article with family members.

Activities:

1. Print a copy of "Activity Page 16.4: Road Signs to Safety" from the CD-ROM. Use these signs while reviewing President Monson's advice. You may also choose to write a brief scenario or two for each sign and see if family members can tell which sign would help them in that specific situation.

2. Print a copy of President Ezra Taft Benson's speech, "Fourteen Fundamentals in Following the Prophet" (available

online on www.lds.org).[133] List each of the fourteen fundamentals on separate slips of paper and place in a container. After reading the above lesson, have family members pull out the slips one at a time to read. Discuss the importance of the point made. Ask how your family can strive to more fully follow the counsel of the living prophet.

Additional Resources:

1. Duane E. Hiatt, author and composer of the song "Follow the Prophet," has penned a verse specifically about President Monson. The new verse is printed in "Follow the Prophet," *Friend*, March 2010, pages 24–25.

2. The nursery manual has a lesson entitled, "I Will Follow the Prophet" (lesson 24). The lesson includes pictures, a coloring activity, a game, and doctrinal instruction.[134]

---

[133] Ezra Taft Benson, "Fourteen Fundamentals in Following the Prophet," *Tambuli*, June 1981, 1.

[134] "Lesson 24: I Will Follow the Prophet," *Behold Your Little Ones: Nursery Manual* (2008), 100–103.

ACTIVITY PAGES ANSWER KEY

Chapter 1: Joseph Smith

Activity Page 1.1: Joseph's Expression of Faith

"The Lord will help me, and I shall get through with it."

Activity Page 1.2: First Vision Crossword Puzzle

Across

2. Air
4. Confused
6. Glory
7. Beloved Son
9. Personages
10. Morning

Down

1. Liberally
3. Fourteen
5. James
8. Grove

Activity Page 1.5: Martyrdom True or False Trivia Quiz

1. True.

2. True.

3. False—Joseph and Hyrum were charged with riot, not disorderly conduct. The Nauvoo City Council felt that the *Nauvoo Expositor* threatened the Saints by inciting mob violence against them. According to rights granted in the Nauvoo Charter, the City Council ruled that the newspaper was a public nuisance and instructed the Prophet, in his role as mayor, to order its destruction.

4. True.

5. False—The reason the warrant (or *mittimus*) was illegal is because it was signed by Justice of the Peace Robert F. Smith even though Joseph and Hyrum had never appeared before him for examination of these charges.

6. False—The jailer and his family lived on the first floor of the jail. There were jail cells on both the first floor and second floor of the building.

7. True.

8. False—In actuality, Governor Ford decided to lead a force of three companies to Nauvoo in an effort to "terrify" the Mormons. All other militias were supposed to be disbanded but they formed a mob instead.

9. False—Joseph had not called up the Nauvoo Legion, but had called for a horse after receiving a letter advising him to go to meet with a lawyer in Quincy.

10. True.

Chapter 2: Brigham Young

Activity Page 2.1: If or If Not

Brigham Young "applied his heart."

Activity Page 2.4: Salt Lake Temple Matching Game

A.—3; B.—1; C.—7; D.—8; E.—6; F.—4; G.—2; H.—5

Chapter 3: John Taylor

Activity Page 3.1: Defenders of the Faith Word Find

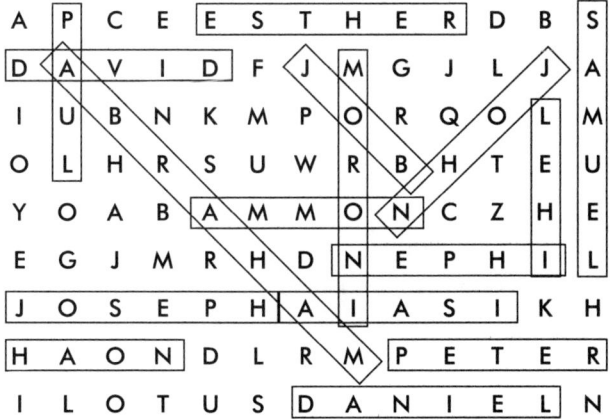

Activity Page 3.2: A Poor Wayfaring Man of Grief

1. A poor, wayfaring Man of grief
Hath often <u>crossed</u> me on my way,
Who <u>sued</u> so humbly for relief
That I could never answer <u>nay</u>.
I had not pow'r to ask his name,
Whereto he went, or <u>whence</u> he came;
Yet there was something in his eye
That won my <u>love</u>; I knew not why.

2. Once, when my <u>scanty</u> meal was spread,
He <u>entered</u>; not a word he spake,
Just perishing for want of <u>bread</u>.
I gave him all; he blessed it, brake,
And ate, but gave me part again.
Mine was an angel's <u>portion</u> then,
For while I fed with eager haste,
The crust was <u>manna</u> to my taste.

3. I spied him where a <u>fountain</u> burst
Clear from the <u>rick</u>; his strength was gone.
The <u>heedless</u> water mocked his thirst;
He heard it, saw it hurrying on.
I ran and raised the suff'rer up;
Thrice from the stream he <u>drained</u> my cup,
Dipped and returned it running o'er;
I drank and never <u>thirsted</u> more.

7. Then in a moment to my view
The stranger started from <u>disguise</u>.
The <u>tokens</u> in his hands I knew;
The Savior <u>stood</u> before mine eyes.
He spake, and my poor name he named,
"Of me thou hast not been <u>ashamed</u>.
These <u>deeds</u> shall thy memorial be;
Fear not, thou didst them unto me."

Chapter 5: Lorenzo Snow

Activity Page 5.2: Prophets Who Have Seen the Lord

	A	B	C	D	E	F	G	H	I	J	K	L
1	█	█									█	█
2	█	█	█							█	█	█
3	█		█							█	█	█
4	█		█						█		█	█
5	█		█						█	█	█	
6	█		█	█				█	█	█		
7	█	█	█						█	█	█	
8	█	█								█	█	
9	█	█							█	█	█	
10	█	█							█	█	█	█
11	█	█	█						█	█	█	█
12	█	█									█	█

Row 1: Alma 19:13—Lamoni
Row 2: 2 Ne. 16:1—Isaiah
Row 3: Ether 12:38–39—Moroni
Row 4: Gen. 32:30—Jacob
Row 5: Abr. 2:6–11—Abraham
Row 6: Ether 3:13, 20—Brother of Jared
Row 7: Ezek. 1:26—Ezekiel
Row 8: 2 Ne. 2:4—Nephi
Row 9: D&C 107:48–49—Enoch
Row 10: JS—H 1:15–20—Joseph Smith
Row 11: Amos 9:1—Amos
Row 12: Ether 9:21–22—Emer

Chapter 6: Joseph F. Smith

Activity Page 6.1: Gifts of the Spirit Word Scramble

1. Wisdom

2. Faith

3. Miracles

4. Angels

5. Tongues

6. Discerning

7. Operations

8. Believe

9. Knowledge

10. Healed

11. Prophesy

12. Ministering

13. Languages

14. Administration

15. Jesus Christ

Activity Page 6.2: Noble and Great Ones Matching Game

1.—K; 2.—N; 3.—C; 4.—L; 5.—I; 6.—G; 7.—A; 8.—E; 9.—J; 10.—M; 11.—B; 12.—D; 13.—F; 14.—H

Activity Page 6.3: Family Fun Nights Crossword

Answers: 1. Perform, 2. Bake, 3. Play music, 4. Visit, 5. Talents, 6. Playing, 7. Thanks, 8. Work, 9. Examine, 10. Lesson, 11. Gardening, 12. Service, 13. Games, 14. Planning, 15. Build, 16. Canning, 17. Singing

Chapter 7: Heber J. Grant

Activity Page 7.1: Scrambled Proverbs

1. There are no shortcuts to any place worth going.

2. There's no substitute for hard work.

3. Where there's a will there's a way.

4. If at first you don't succeed: try, try again.

5. Don't take no for an answer.

6. Rome wasn't built in a day.

7. All things are difficult before they are easy.

8. Make hay while the sun shines.

9. Money doesn't grow on trees.

10. Necessity is the mother of invention.

11. Nothing is impossible to a willing heart.

12. When the going gets tough, the tough get going.

Activity Page 7.2: Heber J. Grant's Two Cents' Worth Puzzle

"If there is any one thing that will bring peace and contentment into the human heart, and into the family, it is to live within our means."[135]

Activity Page 7.3: Word of Wisdom Word Circles

1. Wheat (healthy choice); 2. Alcohol (unhealthy choice); 3. Coffee (unhealthy choice); 4. Grains (healthy choice); 5. Fruits (healthy choice); 6. Tobacco (unhealthy choice)

---

[135] *Gospel Standards: Selections from the Writings and Sermons of Heber J. Grant,* comp. G. Homer Durham (Salt Lake City: Deseret Book Company, 1941), 111.

Chapter 8: George Albert Smith

Activity Page 8.1: George Albert Smith's Personal Creed Word Find

A	E	J	M	Q	U	Y	T	L	M	A	N	K	I	N	D	E	R	S	D	E
C	F	R	I	E	N	D	R	U	B	F	H	I	N	K	O	M	L	P	H	C
L	L	A	P	R	W	R	U	S	E	F	X	D	R	C	F	T	V	G	L	I
R	A	S	O	R	M	S	T	Z	B	L	E	S	S	I	N	G	A	W	P	O
W	T	D	I	I	N	T	H	N	Y	I	N	Q	B	E	V	L	O	S	T	J
S	T	F	U	N	B	L	R	L	R	C	A	E	E	N	K	I	P	L	X	E
O	E	G	Y	G	V	N	T	S	H	T	Y	K	C	E	C	O	A	A	S	R
K	R	H	T	E	C	E	K	A	T	E	Y	M	E	M	I	R	T	E	N	E
G	Y	J	R	K	X	W	O	U	N	D	L	I	N	Y	U	E	L	D	T	A
C	D	P	R	I	V	I	L	E	G	E	B	T	Z	V	R	N	I	I	F	B

Chapter 9: David O. McKay

Activity Page 9.1: Happiness in the Home Hidden Maze

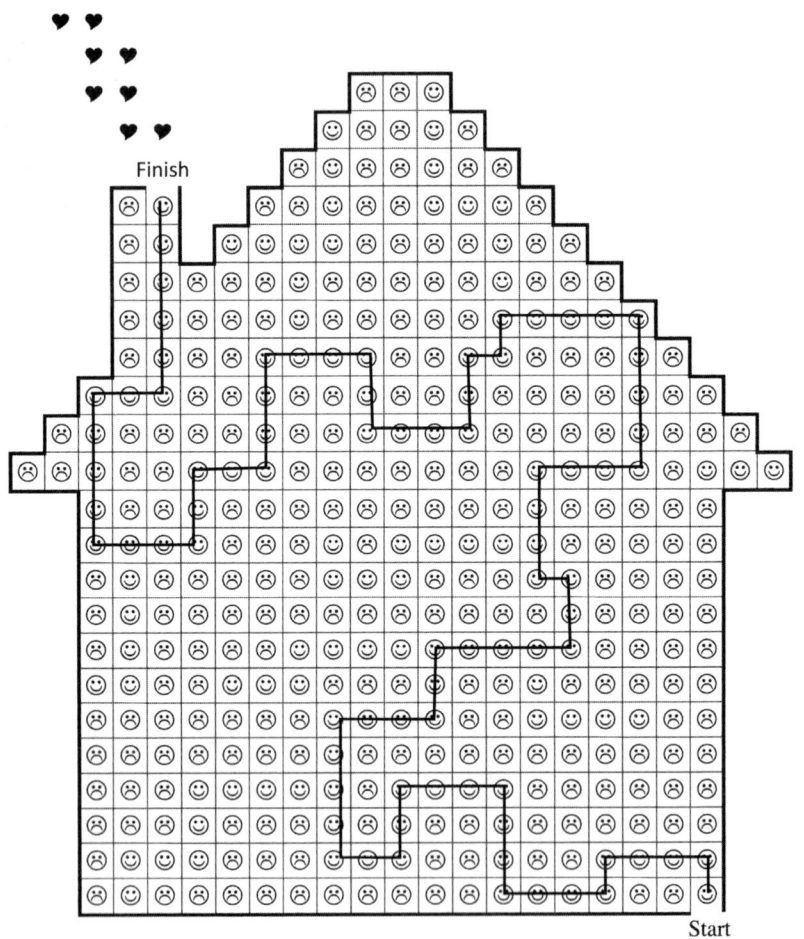

Activity Page 9.2: Seek Learning

1. Astronomy; 2. Archeology; 3. Geology; 4. History; 5. Journalism; 6. Economics; 7. Family Studies; 8. Arts & Humanities; 9. Military Science; 10. International Relations; 11. Law; 12. Political Science

Chapter 10: Joseph Fielding Smith

Activity Page 10.1: Scripture Study Scripture Chase

A. Deut. 6:6–7; B. 2 Ne. 4:15; C. D&C 1:37; D. Rom. 15:4; E. Isa. 34:16; F. D&C 26:1; G. John 5:39; H. 3 Ne. 10:14

Activity Page 10.2: Signs of the Times

1. Promise; 2. Plates of brass; 3. Everlasting gospel; 4. Judah; 5. Suddenly, temple; 6. Wax cold; 7. Wars and rumors of wars; 8. New Jerusalem; 9. Mountains; 10. Destructions; 11. Blossom as a rose; 12. Judah, hand

Chapter 11: Harold B. Lee

Activity Page 11.1: Blessings of Keeping the Commandments

1. H; 2. J; 3. I; 4. B; 5. K; 6. E; 7. A; 8. D; 9. L; 10. G; 11.

C; 12. F

Chapter 12: Spencer W. Kimball

Activity Page 12.3: Who Am I?

1. Nephi; 2. Joseph; 3. Prodigal Son; 4. Pahoran

Chapter 13: Ezra Taft Benson

Activity Page 13.1: Ottendorf Pride Cipher

"Pride is the great stumbling block to Zion." —Ezra Taft Benson

Chapter 14: Howard W. Hunter

Activity Page 14.1: Musical Instrument Puzzler

1. Drum; 2. Piano; 3. Harmonica; 4. Trumpet; 5. Bagpipe; 6. Oboe; 7. Organ; 8. Bass; 9. Tuba; 10. Bugle; 11. Harp; 12. Banjo

Activity Page 14.3: Christ-Centered Maze

Chapter 15: Gordon B. Hinckley

Activity Page 15.3: Temple Expertise

Salt Lake Temple, 2. Nauvoo Illinois Temple, 3. Laie Hawaii Temple, 4. Hong Kong China Temple, 5. Mexico City Mexico Temple, 6. Bern Switzerland Temple.

Chapter 16: Thomas S. Monson

Activity Page 16.1: Homing Pigeon Maze

Finish

Start

Activity Page 16.2: Secret Service Message

"Fill your life with service." —Thomas S. Monson